Japanese: The Written Language
Part 1
Field Test Edition

Eleanor Harz Jorden and Mari Noda

 Cheng & Tsui Company

2019 printing

23 22 21 20 19   13 14 15
13th Printing

Cheng & Tsui Company
25 West Street
Boston, Massachusetts 02111-1268 USA

Please send your comments to:

Mari Noda
Department of East Asian Languages and Literatures
The Ohio State University
204 Cunz Hall, 1841 Millikin Rd.
Columbus, OH 43210-1229

Printed in the United States of America

TABLE OF CONTENTS

LESSON 1

INTRODUCTION

The first four lessons introduce *katakana*, the syllabary used primarily for writing loan words (i.e., words borrowed from foreign languages). *Katakana* is also used to represent native Japanese items that are intended to stand out in the context in which they occur. The use of *katakana* in Japanese often corresponds to the use of italics in English: *katakana* occurs frequently in advertisements; it is also used in writing items that represent something strange or unusual from a linguistic point of view (for example in quoting foreigners' errors in Japanese); and it is often used in writing onomatopoeic words -- i.e., those that are supposed to represent their meaning by their sound (example: *gatagata*, representing a rattling sound). In addition, *katakana* is used in writing telegrams and, together with Chinese characters (kanzi), in writing legal documents.

Ideally, students of Japanese as a foreign language begin to learn to read Japanese having already gained some knowledge of the spoken language, even if very limited. After all, a written language is basically a representation of the oral. Therefore, it is important to remember the order that is implied: spoken then written -- as all native speakers of every language in the world know in connection with their own language.

Most English-speaking students of Japanese begin their study of the language with some use of romanization,[1] introduced not as a writing system but as a study aid, a reminder of the spoken language which is being orally practiced and drilled. We will, therefore, introduce *katakana* symbols with reference to their equivalents in romanization, on the assumption that students have already learned the appropriate Japanese pronunciation

---

[1] The romanization used in this text will be identical with that used in JSL except that /g/ and /ḡ/ will not be distinguished. The simple /g/ will be used as a cover symbol for both.

represented by the romanized symbols. For the student who has not had such an introduction, it will be particularly important to listen to the oral representation of these symbols (either by hearing them read by a native speaker or by listening to a tape recording of them), and to read a description of them in the Introduction to *Japanese: The Spoken Language* (hereafter JSL). We must always remember that the sounds of Japanese are not the same as the sounds of English, even if a few of them are similar.

The major adjustment that native speakers of English must make in learning to read and write *katakana* is to move from an alphabetic system to a syllabic system -- or, more accurately, a mora-representing system. While there are many exceptions in both English and Japanese -- particularly in English -- in general, we think of English writing as one which is basically one-sound-one-letter, whereas the Japanese usually writes *katakana* in terms of one-beat(mora)-one-symbol.

For example, if we take the names 'Nina' and 'Lisa' as examples, English speakers hear 4 sounds in each. We also hear similar vowel sequences in the 2 names and use the same letters /i/ and /a/ to represent them. What is more, we hear the consonant /n/ twice in the first name, and therefore expect the same letter to occur twice in its spelling.

But what about the *katakana* representation? Each name is written by mora (= the syllable-like Japanese units that each represent one beat) and therefore no symbol will occur twice in the writing of these two names: nothing in the writing will suggest either the resemblance in the vowels or the occurrence of /n/ twice in 'Nina.' The first symbol for 'Nina' will represent /ni/, and the last, totally different symbol, will represent /na/. 'Lisa' will also be represented by different symbols, one standing for the /li/ and another for the /sa/.

To sum up: All symbols that represent the two names will represent entire mora and will be different: there will be no suggestion in the symbols themselves that the same vowels /i/ and /a/ occur in both names, or that the consonant /n/ occurs twice in 'Nina.'

Our first task is now to learn the *katakana* symbols that represent the mora of Japanese. When Japanese children, already fluent in the spoken language, learn to read, they begin with a different set of mora-representing-symbols, called *hiragana*, for reasons that simply do not apply to the foreign learner. For us, *katakana* has definite advantages as the first system to master. From the start, we want to read and write in authentic, adult style, and to begin by using *hiragana* to represent everything in the language is not the way Japanese normally write. In fact, starting in the first grade, Japanese children begin to use Chinese characters (*kanzi*) together with their *hiragana*. What is more, there is very little we can read or write in *hiragana* that we understand, assuming that we begin our study of the Japanese writing system when we have only a very limited knowledge of the language: we definitely want to begin our work in written Japanese with a large quantity of material that is immediately familiar.

Since words borrowed from Western languages (especially English) are regularly written in *katakana*, we have an extensive inventory available. *Katakana* immediately provides us with a wealth of material that we can handle and that can be written authentically. What is more, it is important that we be reminded of the diference between the Japanese and English sound systems, and *katakana* provides excellent practice as we transfer directly from one language to the other. Finally, knowledge of *katakana* alone enables us to read many authentic samples from Japan, from restaurant menus to hotel accommodations; *hiragana* alone has little use. We will therefore begin with *katakana*, then add *hiragana* and work with examples that use both of these syllabaries (known collectively as *kana*), and inally add *kanzi*. At all times, we will always be working with the language written authentically, in normal adult style.

There are. of course, loanwords in the Japanese language that have come from lnguages other than English. However, the vast majority have English origins and it is these on which we will focus most of our attention.

We can make a general statement to the effect that it is possible for the Japanese to use *katakana* to represent English. But this must never be equated with the use of romanization to represent Japanese. In katakana, everything is written and read according to the pronunciation rules of Japanese; in many cases, an English borrowing, pronounced in *katakana* style, is incomprehensible to a native speaker of English, particularly one who knows no Japanese language. Romanization, on the other hand, is a code for using Roman letters to represent the accurate pronunciation of a foreign language. *Ohayoo gozaimasu* represents the accurate, native Japanese pronunciation of a Japanese sequence. In contrast, *katakana*-style *guddo-mooningu* 'good morning,' represents English pronounced AS IF IT WERE JAPANESE. Thus, romanization represents, in Roman letters, true native-style pronunciation of the Japanese language (or any other language), whereas *katakana* represents Japanese-style pronunciation of English (or any other language).[2]

Items borrowed from English and written in *katakana* can almost always be uderstood by the native speaker of English, provided a few rules of conversion are learned. And once having heard the Japanese borrowing of a foreign word, it is almost invariably possible to write it accurately in *katakana*, once the symbols have been learned. (Could we say this about the predictability of English spelling???)

However, given an English word in its original form, we cannot always predict what the Japanese conversion will be: borrowings in Japanese are usually based on English or American pronunciation, but sometimes on

2. There are some languages that have adopted an official romanized writing system in place of a traditional system that used totally different symbols. Vietnamese is an example.

English spelling, and there is no way to make foolproof predictions for any individual case; what is more, there are often a number of different pronunciations occurring in English and there is no way to predict which one the Japanese have chosen as the basis for their borrowing. We will therefore concentrate our efforts on how to *read katakana* and how to *write borrowed words* in Japanese. We will not be expected to move from English directly to Japanese when the borrowed Japanese word is unfamiliar. However, as we gain more and more experience in reading *katakana* and note the conversions from English to Japanese that have already been made, we will find that we are automatically gaining the added facility of predicting with considerable even if not perfect accuracy how to move in this opposite direction.

Consider, for a moment, the question of pronunciation vs. spelling. In studying the spoken language, we learn the Japanese borrowing for 'cake.' We represent this borrowing in romanization as *keeki*. The *katakana* writing of this word, with three symbols representing *ke-e-ki*, corresponds to its Japanese pronunciation (and romanization), NOT its English spelling. In learning to read *katakana*, it is important always to pronounce an item aloud and listen, since most borrowings are based on pronunciation. We must not get entangled in the vagaries of English spelling until we recognize the English item that is represented.

We will now begin to master *katakana*, learning each symbol within the context of occurring items, and remembering always to learn to read first (the receptive skill), then to write (the productive skill). We will be concerned with learning the *katakana* representation for each of the 113 mora of Japanese plus a few special conventions that occur only in borrowed words pronounced with innovative pronunciation.

Henceforth we will use the following conventions: English glosses will be enclosed in single quotation marks ('cake'); romanization will be represented with italics (*keeki*); and lower case letters enclosed in slashes will represent sounds as in English (/k/) or occasionally as in another specified foreign language. A romanized vowel preceded by a hyphen (as in -*e*) represents both the mora consisting of the vowel alone (*e*) as well as any mora ending in the vowel (*ke*, *se*, *te*, etc.). Remember that in *katakana* writing, there will be a single unit symbol for each different /consonant + vowel/ combination; the consonant and vowel cannot be written separately as they can in romanization.

First, it is useful to master the regular vowel correspondences. The following list covers most conversions. All Japanese vowels and vowel combinations occur both with or without a preceding consonant, hence the hyphen preceding each Japanese item below.

Japanese:	corresponds to the English vowel or diphthong[3] of:
-*a*	'pat' or 'pad' or 'put'
-*aa*	'ma'
-*ai*	'my'
-*au* or -*ao*	'cow'
-*i*	'sit' (or 'seat')
-*ii*	'seed'
-*u*	'look' (or 'Luke')
-*uu*	'mood'
-e	'let' (or 'late')
-*ee* or -*ei*	'laid'
-*o*	'cot' (or 'coat')
-*oo*	'mode' or 'Maud'
-*ou*	'mode'
-*oi*	'boy'

3. A diphthong is a combination of several vowel sounds within one syllable. For example, English 'high' is a one-syllable word containing a diphthong that moves from an /a/-sound to an /ee/-sound. Compare the pronunciation of Japanese *hai*, which has two mora (*ha* + *i*) rather than one diphthong.

KATAKANA SYMBOLS

We will begin by reading English-language given names, both male and female, as they have been borrowed into the Japanese language. Besides their frequent occurrence in the Japanese media, these are often found on the *meesi* (calling cards) of foreigners in Japan.

As a start, how is the name 'Nina' represented in the Japanese writing system?

Actually this name is pronounced with its first vowel lengthened, giving us a third mora: NI-I-NA.

The katakana symbol: corresponds to romanized: Handwritten Equivalents[4]

1 二   *ni*

2 ナ   *na*

Japanese may be written horizontally, usually from left to right,[5] or vertically, from top to bottom.

A special symbol, which occurs commonly in *katakana*, is:

▬   in horizontal writing

and

│ in vertical writing,

---

4. The righthand symbol indicates how each stroke is written, i.e., the stroke order and the direction of each stroke.

5. On moving vehicles -- on the sides of ships, taxicabs, etc. -- we find examples of right-to-left, horizontal writing.

representing the lengthening of the vowel of the preceding mora. It takes up one full space.

We can now write the Japanese equivalent of 'Nina':

ニ ー ナ   or: ニ
                                  |
                                  ナ   *Niina*

Japanese writing is best practiced on boxed paper, with each symbol assigned one box. Remember that, when reading it, the pronunciation must be Japanese-style, always different from English pronunciation.

Now, how is 'Lisa' represented in *katakana*? Since the vowels are both heard as short, only two symbols will be used, one representing /li/ and the other /sa/. But there is nothing in our chart of the 113 mora of Japanese that corresponds to /li/. What is actually used is the closest there is, namely the mora represented in romanization as /ri/. We now can state our first conversion rule for converting borrowed Japanese back to English.

CONVERSION RULE 1:
The /r-/ that begins a mora may represent an English /r/ or /l/, even though this Japanese sound is different from both these English sounds.

3 リ   *ri*

4 サ   *sa*

We are now ready to write 'Lisa' in katakana:

リ サ　　　　　or:　　　　リ
　　　　　　　　　　　　　サ　　　　*Lisa*

Can you read the following names? Remember not to be confused by English spelling: most conversion is based on pronunciation.

a. リー　　　　　　　*Rii*　　　'Lee'
b. リ リー　　　　　　*Riri*　　'Lilly'
c. サ リー　　　　　　*Sarii*　　'Sally'

We will now add to our *katakana* symbols and conversion rules, continuing to use given names as our borrowing category.

5 テ　　　　*te*

occurs in:
テ リー　　　　　　　*terii*　　'Terry' or 'Telly'

6 ン　　　　*ñ*

This symbol represents the syllabic nasal of Japanese: in word- final position, it converts to an /n/ in English; elsewhere it converts to sounds similar to /m/, /n/, or /ng/, depending on the following sound, parallel to its regular pronunciation in Japanese.

Example
リ ン　　　　　　　　*Riñ*　　'Lynn'

7 ア　　　　*a*

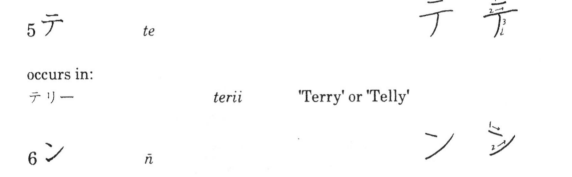

This *kakakana* symbol occurs only when /a/ represents an entire mora, NOT when it occurs as the vowel of a mora consisting of a /consonant + a/ like /na/, or when it represents lengthening of the preceding vowel (represented by a straight line).

Examples
a. アン   *An*   'Ann(e)'
b. リリアン   *Ririañ*   'Lillian'

8 ト   *to*   ト ⺊

occurs in:
トニー   *Tonii*   'Tony'

9 ム   *mu*   ム ⺈

In English, unlike Japanese, many words and syllables end in a consonant. (In Japanese, only a nasal consonant, represented by syllabic /n/, may occur in this position.) When borrowing into Japanese items with a final consonant that is not /n/, the most common procedure is to add /u/, i.e., to use a /consonant + u/ mora. This gives us our second conversion rule:

CONVERSION RULE 2:
In converting from Japanese back to English, try omitting occurrences of the /u/ vowel that follow consonants at the end of words and syllables.

Examples:
a. トム   *Tomu*   'Tom'
b. サム   *Samu*   'Sam'

10 ケ   *ke*   ケ ⺹

What names are these?

a. ケン		*Ken*	'Ken'
b. ケニー		*Kenii*	'Kenny'
c. ケリー		*Kerii*	'Kelly'

The /t + u/ combination in Japanese regularly has a pronunciation similar to English /tsu/, which makes it quite different from English /tu/. Thus, to represent /t/ at the end of English words or syllables, instead of following the usual /add u/ rule, Japanese usually uses /to/.

CONVERSION RULE 3:

When converting from Japanese back to English, try dropping the /o/ of the mora /to/ when it occurs at the end of an English word or syllable.

Thus:

ケート	*Keeto*	'Kate'

11 ロ   *ro*   ロ ロ

Can you read these names?

a. ロン		*Roñ*	'Ron'
b. ロニー		*Ronii*	'Ronny'
c. ローリー		*Roorii*	'Laurie'

12 ス   *su*   ス ズ

occurs in:

a. スー	*Suu*	'Sue'
b, アリス	*Arisu*	'Alice'

13 ク   *ku*   ク グ

Consonant clusters (= sequences of consonants within a single syllable, as in 'street'), a common feature of English, are impossible in Japanese. The usual procedure is to convert from English by using mora that end in /u/ (or, if the consonant is /t/, the mora /to/), for all except the syllabic nasal /n/ and the final consonant of the cluster. Thus, 'street,' converted into Japanese, becomes ストリート *sutoriito*. In moving back from Japanese to English, once again we try dropping occurrences of /u/ in /consonant + u/ mora and the /o/ of /to/, just as we did when these examples occurred at the end of a word or syllable (Conversion Rules 2 and 3).

Example

クリス	*Kurisu*	'Chris'

14 ル   *ru*   ル リレ

occurs in:

a.	ルー	*Ruu* '	Lew' or 'Lou'
b.	ルーク	*Ruuku* '	Luke'

15 マ   *ma*   マ マ

Can you identify these names?

a.	マリー	*Marii*	'Marie'
b.	マリア	*Maria*	'Maria';
c.	トーマス	*Toomasu*	'Thomas'

The combinations /ar/ as in 'hard' and /er/ as in 'herd'[6] in English are usually represented in Japanese as a long /-*aa*/, or sometimes as a short /-*a*/ in word-

---

6. Note the variety of English spellings that represent these sounds, in words such as 'her', 'sir', 'fur', 'purr', 'word'.

final position. Unpredictably the combination may also be represented according to the more general pattern as /-aru/ and /-eru/.

CONVERSION RULE 4:

Check any occurrences of /-aa/ (and also /-a/ in word-final position) for possible representation of English /ar/ or /er/.

Thus:

マーク	Maaku	'Mark'

The /th/ sound, as in English 'thank,' does not occur in Japanese. As a replacement, Japanese usually use a mora beginning with /s/. Thus, 'thank' is converted to Japanese サンク sanku, which could of course also represent English 'sank.'

CONVERSION RULE 5:

An /s/ may convert back to English as an /s/ or a /th/ as in 'thank'.

Do you recognize these names?

a. マーサ	Maasa	'Martha'
b. アーサー	Aasaa	'Arthur'
c. ルース	Ruusu	'Ruth'

16 イ   *i*   イ 㐅

This is another example of a *katakana* symbol that represents a vowel alone as a mora. It occurs only when the vowel /i/ is a mora by itself and is not the lengthening of the vowel of the preceding mora (represented by a line).

Can you read these names?

a. イアン	Iañ	'Ian'
b. ロイ	Roi	'Roy'
c. リーロイ	Riiroi	'Leroy'

d. ルイ	*Rui*	'Louie'
e. ルイス	*Ruisu'*	Louis' or 'Lewis'

The English diphthong /ay/ as in 'May' may be borrowed either with a long /-ee/ or /-ei/ in Japanese loanwords. In some examples, only one of these spellings is regularly used, and in others, we have a choice.

Thus:

ケート	*Keeto*	
or		
ケイト	*Kei to*	'Kate'

17 シ   *si*

If we recall all the romanized mora that begin with /s/, we note that there is a noticeable change in the quality of the sound represented by /s/ when it occurs before /i/, bringing it closer to (but NOT THE SAME AS!) English /sh/. It is not surprising, then, that both 'see' and 'she' are written in the same way when converted to Japanese: シー *sii*

CONVERSION RULE 6:
The /s/ in the mora /si/ may represent English /s/ or /sh/ or, as previously pointed out, /th/.

What personal names are these?

a. シーナ	*Siina*	'Sheena'
b. シリア	*Siria*	'Celia'
c. シシリア	*Sisiria*	'Cecelia'
d. ナンシー	*Nañsii*	'Nancy'
e. マーシー	*Maasii*	'Marcy'
f. ルーシー	*Ruusii*	'Ruthie'

18 レ   *re*   レ   ⟱

Can you read these names?

a.	アレン	*Aren*	'Allen'
b.	クレア	*Kurea*	'Clair'
c.	レスリー	*Resurii*	'Lesley'
d.	ローレン	*Rooreñ*	'Lauren'
e.	ローレンス	*Rooreñsu*	'Lawrence'
f.	トレーシー	*Toreesii*	'Tracy'
g.	テレサ	*Teresa'*	Teresa'
h.	レー	*Ree*	

or

       レイ   *Rei*   'Ray'

19 ヘ   *he*   ヘ   ⌃

What are these names?

a.	ヘンリー	*Heñrii*	'Henry'
b.	ヘレン	*Hereñ*	'Helen'
c.	ヘレナ	*Helena*	'Helena'

20 エ   *e*   

Here, again, is a symbol that represents a vowel alone. It is used only when /e/ occurs as a mora by itself, although never to represent lengthening of a preceding vowel (represented by a straight line).

Examples:

a.	エマ	*Ema*	'Emma'
b.	エレン	*Ereñ*	'Ellen'

c. エ リ ン	*Eriñ*	'Erin'
d. エ ル シ ー	*Erusii*	'Elsie'

A /ye/ sequence at the beginning of a word has traditionally been represented by /ee/ or /ie/.

Example:

エ ー ル	*yeeru*	

or

イ エ ー ル	ieeru	'Yale'

Conversion Rule 7:
When converting a Japanese initial /ee/ or /ie/, try /ye/ as the foreign equivalent.

REVIEW

REVIEW 1: Predictably the names for foreign foods and drinks are borrowed into Japanese along with the actual items. Can you read and identify these examples? Remember to retain the Japanese pronunciation when you are reading![7]

a. ト マ ト	_____	b. ト ー ス ト	_____
c. ロ ー ス ト	_____	d. シ リ ア ル	_____
e. ク リ ー ム	_____	f. ア イ ス ク リ ー ム	_____

REVIEW 2: Now read the following list of *katakana* words, identifying: (1). a holiday; (2). two U.S. presidents; (3). a type of pastry; (4). two sports; (5). a make of car; (6). two country names; and (7). three city names.

a. ト ロ イ	b. ト ル ー マ ン
c. ア イ ス ス ケ ー ト	d. ル ー マ ニ ア
e. ク リ ン ト ン	f. ク リ ス マ ス

7. You can check your answers using the answer key at the end of Lesson 1.

g. リマ   h. ロシア

i. エクレア   j. ロールスロイス

k. テニス   l. シアトル

Before going on to Lesson 2, review all the examples of Lesson 1, making certain that you are able to read with facility every one of the twenty *katakana* symbols that have been introduced. Reading *katakana* even in context provides only limited opportunity for guessing symbols you don't know. YOU MUST BE SURE OF THE SOUND VALUE OF ALL THE SYMBOLS.

Note those symbols that have rather similar shapes:

ア and マ and ム;   レ and ル

Whenever you encounter difficulties in figuring out how to convert a *katakana* item, try writing out its romanized equivalent and then apply the conversion rules. This should be necessary on only rare occasions, but remember it as a fallback position.

SUMMARY

Examine now the chart of Japanese mora as it is traditionally written (in rows beginning on the right, in the order indicated), with the symbols you have learned in Lesson 1 inserted in appropriate boxes. This 10 X 5 chart is regularly referred to as the table of *gozyuuon* '50 sounds', even though not all the boxes are filled and syllabic /n̄/ is an 'extra'.

ン ñ	wa	ra	ya	マ ma	ha	ナ na	ta	サ sa	ka	ア a
		リ ri		mi	hi	ニ ni	ti	シ si	ki	イ i
		ル ru	yu	ム mu	hu	nu	tu	ス su	ク ku	u
		レ re		me	ヘ he	ne	テ te	se	ケ ke	エ e
		ロ ro	yo	mo	ho	no	ト to	so	ko	o

ABOUT WRITING PRACTICE

The first task with *katakana* is to become able to recognize the symbols quickly and accurately. Pay special attention to the features that distinguish one symbol from another, like the direction of the strokes, relative length of the strokes, and the position of the strokes. Writing the symbols helps you retain the shape in your mind. The following practice is intended only as a way to help you learn to produce these symbols. Hold off on the practice of writing items in katakan until you can read with relative ease those items written in katakana.

To practice writing the symbols, use the models presented on the next two pages. and follow these procedures:

(1)   Place a sheet of tracing paper or airmail letter paper over the model.

(2)   Trace the completed symbol. Refer to the frames from left to right so that you follow the proper stroke order and that you are using the right kind of stroke.

(3) Go to the next frame, which is one stroke short of being complete. Trace the entire symbol again, filling in the missing stroke.

(4) Continue moving left one frame at a time, each time writing a complete symbol by filling in the mising strokes until you get to the left-most fram where you will be filling in every stroke except the ifrst one. Practice writing the entire symbol by yourwelf using boxed paper.

Remember that your practice at this point is limited to production of individual symbols. As you begin reading *hiragana*, you should start writing words that are ordinarily written in *katakana*.

KATAKANA WRITING PRACTICE

	1	2	
ni	一	二	
	1	**2**	
na	一	ナ	
	1		**1**
length	一	or	I
	1	**2**	
ri	l	リ	
	1	**2**	**3**
sa	一	十	サ
	1	**2**	**3**
te	一	二	テ
	1	**2**	
n	`	ン	
	1	**2**	
a	フ	ア	
	1	**2**	
to	l	ト	

	1	2	
mu	ム	ム	
	1	**2**	**3**
ke	ノ	ト	ケ
	1	**2**	**3**
ro	l	ロ	ロ
	1	**2**	
su	フ	ス	
	1	**2**	
ku	ノ	ク	
	1	**2**	
ru	ノ	ル	
	1	**2**	
ma	フ	マ	
	1	**2**	
i	ノ	イ	
	1	**2**	**3**
si	`	二	シ

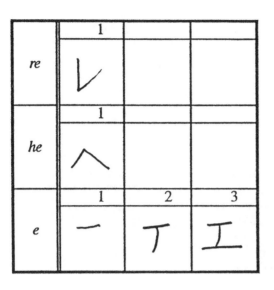

ANSWER KEY

Review 1.
a. *tomato* 'tomato'; b. *toosuto* 'toast'; c. *roosuto* 'roast'; d. *siriaru* 'cereal';
e. *kuriimu* 'cream'; f. *aisukuriim* 'ice cream'

Review 2
(1). a holiday: f. クリスマス (*Kurisumasu* 'Christmas')
(2). two U.S. presidents: b. トルーマン (*Toruumañ* 'Truman');
                         e. クリントン (*Kurintoñ* 'Clinton')
(3). a type of pastry: i. エクレア (*ekurea* 'eclair')
(4). two sports: c. アイススケート (*aisusukeeto* 'ice skat(ing)');
                         k. テニス (*tenisu* 'tennis')
(5). a make of car: . ロールスロイス (*Roorusuroisu* 'Rolls Royce')
(6). two country names; d. ルーマニア (*Ruumania* 'Rumania');
                         h. ロシア (*Rosia* 'Russia')
(7). three city names: トロイ (*Toroi* 'Troy'); g. リマ (*Rima* 'Lima');
                         l. シアトル (*Siatoru* 'Seattle')

LESSON 2

REVIEW

With the exception of names of places in Japan and of a few in the rest of Asia, place names have been borrowed by the Japanese from foreign languages. These are all written in *katakana*, which, as usual, may be derived from the foreign spelling rather than the pronunciation. The origin may be English or another foreign language.1

REVIEW 1: Can you read these place names? (Several were included in Review 2 at the end of Lesson 1.)

a. リマ　　　　　_____　　b. ローマ　　　　　_____

c. ニース　　　　_____　　d. スイス　　　　　_____

e. ロシア　　　　_____　　f. シリア　　　　　_____

g. シアトル　　　_____　　h. マレーシア　　　_____

i. ルーマニア　　_____

****

Now we will increase our inventory of symbols.

KATAKANA SYMBOLS (cont.)

21 ワ　　　　*wa*　　　　　　　　　　ワ　ヴ

Examples:
Another place-name:

1. See Answer Key at the end of this lesson to check your answers.

a. ワシントン   *wasiñtoñ* 'Washington'

and some additional given-names:

b. ワリー   *warii* 'Wally'

c. ワレス   *waresu* 'Wallace'

22 ハ   *ha*

ハ ＼ ﾊ ハ

Examples:

Where?

a. ハワイ   *hawai* 'Hawaii'

Who?

b. ハナ   *Hana* 'Hannah'

c. ハリー   *Harii* 'Harry'

23 ラ   *ra*

ラ ﾗ

Examples:

Where?

a. イラク   *iraku* 'Iraq'

b. マニラ   *manira* 'Manila'

Who?

c. エラ   *era*   'Ella'

d. ラリー   *Rarii* 'Larry'

e. シーラ   *Siira* 'Sheila'

24 カ   *ka*

カ 力

Examples:

Where?

a. カイロ   *Kairo* 'Cairo';

b. アラスカ   *Arasuka* 'Alaska'

Who?

c. カール	*Kaaru*	'Karl'
d. カロライナ	*karoraina'*	

or

カロリーナ	*karoriina*	'Carolina'

25 メ　　　　　*me*　　　　　　　　　　　　　　メ　　メ

Examples:

Where?

a. メイン	*Meiñ*	'Maine'
b. アメリカ	*Amerika*	'America'

Who?

c. メー	*Mee*	

or

メイ	*Mei*	'May'
d. メリー	*Merii*	

or

メリー	*Mearii*	'Mary'

What greeting do we frequently hear in December?

メリー・クリスマス	*Merii Kurisumasu*	'Merry Christmas'

The raised dot is used in *katakana* to separate parts of a sequence. It occurs frequently between the given (and middle) and family names in a Western name, as in: ハリー・ハリス *Harii Harisu* 'Harry Harris'; メリー・アン・リー *Merii An Rii* 'Mary Ann Lee.' Note that the Japanese retain the regular Western-style order of /given name(s) + family name/ when transferring a Western name to the Japanese language, even though the order for native Japanese names is the opposite. Sometimes the dot occurs within what would be considered a single compound word in English. For example, don't be surprised to find examples like 'straw berry.' All in all, its use is quite erratic and unpredictable.)

26 夕   *ta*   夕 夕

Examples:
Where?

| a. TAI | *Tai* | 'Thai(land)' |
| b. イタリア | *Itaria* | 'Italy' |

Who?

c. リタ	*Rita*	'Rita'
d. アニタ	*Anita*	'Anita'
e. スタンリー	*Sutañrii*	'Stanley'

27 フ   *hu*   フ フ

This mora is used to represent both /hu/ and /fu/ in foreign words, since it is the closest approximation there is in Japanese to both.

CONVERSION RULE 8:

In converting the mora /*hu*/, try both /hu/ and /fu/ as possible foreign equivalents. Note フー 'who?' and フレー *huree* 'hooray' as well as:

Place-names:

| a. フランス | *Hurañsu* | 'France' |
| b. アフリカ | *Ahurika* | 'Africa' |

Given-names:

c. フランク	*Hurañku*	'Frank'
d. フランシス	*Hurañsisu*	'Francis'
e. ルーフス	*Ruuhusu*	'Rufus'
f. フローレンス	*Huroreñsu*	'Florence'

28 ノ   *no*   ノ   ノ

Examples:

Where?

a. ノーム   *Noomu*   'Nome'

Who?

b. ノア   *Noa*   'Noah'

c. ノラ   *Nora*   'Nora'

When an English /-or/ occurs before a consonant (for example, 'Norman'), it is usually transferred into Japanese as /-oo/ (ノーマン *Noomañ*). Alternatively the /-or/ may be converted into /-oru/, following the more general rule (ノルマン *Norumañ*). However, when /-or/ occurs at the end of the word (for example, 'Eleanor'), we regularly find /-oa/ in the Japanese equivalent (エレノア *Erenoa* or エリノア *Erinoa*).

CONVERSION RULE 9:

A long /-oo/ vowel followed by a mora beginning with a consonant may convert to an /or/ in English. In word-final position, Japanese /-oa/ may also convert to /or/.

These conversions are similar to those introduced in Conversion Rule 4, in Lesson 1.

Examples:

Where?

d. ノースアメリカ   *Noosuamerika* 'North America'

e. ノースカロライナ   *Noosukaroraina*   'North Carolina'

Who?

f. ノーマ   *Nooma*

or

    ノルマ   *Noruma*   'Norma'

g. ノーマン　　　　　*Noomañ*

or

　ノルマン　　　　　*Norumañ*　'Norman

h. エレノア　　　　　*Erenoa*

or

　エリノア　　　　　*Erinoa*　'Eleanor' (in its various English spellings)

29 オ　　　　　o　　　　　　　　　　　　　才　才

Here again is a symbol that represents a mora consisting of a vowel alone: in this case, the vowel is /o/ as a mora -- not as the lengthening of the preceding vowel (for which the symbol is a straight line) and not as the final vowel of a mora consisting of /consonant + o/.

Examples:

Place-names:

a. オタワ　　　　　*Otawa*　　　'Ottawa'

b. ラオス　　　　　*Raosu*　　　'Laos'

c. オハイオ　　　　*Ohaio*　　　'Ohio'

d. アイオワ　　　　*Aiowa*　　　'Iowa'

e. オーストリア　　*Oosutoria*　'Austria'

f. オーストラリア　*Oosutoraria* 'Australia'

Given-names:

g. オスカー　　　　*Osukaa*　　'Oscar'

h. マリオン　　　　*Marioñ*　　'Marion'

30 ミ　　　　　mi　　　　　　　　　　　　ニ　ミ

Examples:

Where?

a. マイアミ   *Maiami* 'Miami'

Who?

b. ミミ   *Mimi*   'Mimi'

c. ナオミ   *Naomi*   'Naomi'

d. ミルトン   *Mirutoñ*   'Milton'

e. ノラ・スミス   *Nora Sumisu*   'Nora Smith'

DIACRITICS

NIGORI

Compare the following pairs of symbols:

カ and ガ;   サ and ザ;   タ and ダ;   ハ and バ

The left-hand members of these pairs are already familiar. They are equivalent to the romanized mora *ka*, *sa*, *ta*, and *ha*. The corresponding symbols on the right are equivalent to the romanized mora *ga*, *za*, *da*, and *ba*. In other words, the addition of / ʺ / (called *nigori*) changes the value of the initial consonant of a mora; /k/ changes to /g/, /s/ to /z/, /t/ to /d/, and /h/ to /b/. Compare: テリー *Terii* 'Telly' (or 'Terry') and デリー *Derii* 'Delhi.'

With the introduction of *nigori*, the number of examples for practice increases tremendously. Be sure to practice reading these examples aloud **WITH JAPANESE-STYLE PRONUNCIATION**. It is important to avoid the common error of switching to English pronunciation as soon as the English origin of a word is recognized.

The following are *katakana* symbols with *nigori* that we can recognize immediately.

ガ   *ga*   ガ ガ

グ　　　　*gu*

ゲ　　　　*ge*

Examples:

Places:

a. ガーナ　　　　　*Gana*　　　'Ghana'

b. ミシガン　　　　*Misigañ*　　'Michigan'

c. アフガニスタン　*Ahuganisutañ*　'Afghanistan'

d. ハンガリー　　　*Hañgarii*　　'Hungary'

People:

e. ガイ　　　　　*Gai*　　　'Guy'

f. オルガ　　　　*Oruga*　　'Olga'

g. グレース　　　*Gureesu*　　'Grace'

h. ギー　　　　　*Gee*

or

ゲイ　　　　　*Gei*　　　'Gay'

i. ゲール　　　　*geeru*

or

ゲイル　　　　*geiru*　　'Gail'

The syllabic nasal /n/ at the end of a word is regularly converted to an /n/ in English. Note that the combination /ngu/ is the usual representation of a word-final /ng/ in English. Once again we are simply dropping a /u/ when we convert from Japanese back to English. Example: サイクリング *saikuringu* 'cycling'

ザ　　　　*za*

ジ　　　*zi*

ズ　　　*zu*

Paralleling the use of /s/ as a conversion for the /th/ of 'thank' in English, /z/ may represent the /th/ of 'this' in addition to its usual transfer for /z/. In addition, since there is no mora in traditional Japanese with pronunciation resembling English /zee/ or /dee/, we find that /zi/ covers for both of these as well as for /jee/. The fourth possibility, the least common, is the /si/ of 'Asia', also coveed by /zi/.

CONVERSION RULE 10:

The consonant /z/ in Japanese may represent the /th/ of 'this' (= ジ ス *zisu*) in English as well as the /z/ of 'zone'. In addition, the mora /zi/ may serve as the conversion of English /zee/, /jee/, /dee/, and, occasionally, of the /si/ of 'Asia.' In word- or syllable-final position, ジ may represent English /j/.

Examples:
Places:

a. カンザス	*Kañzasu*	'Kansas'
b. アジア	*Azia*	'Asia';
c. ミ ズ ー リ	*Mizuuri*	'Missouri'

People:

d. ザカ リ ー	*Zakarii*	'Zachary'
e. ス ー ザ ン	*Suuzañ*	'Susan'
f. ヘザー	*Hezaa*	'Heather'
g. ジ ミ ー	*Zimii*	'Jimmy'
h. ジ ム	*Zimu*	'Jim'
i. ジ ー ン	*Ziiñ*	'Jean'
j. ジ ル	*ziru*	'Jill'

k. ジーク	*Ziiku*	'Zeke'
l. ローズ	*Roozu*	'Rose'
m. ルイーズ	*Ruiizu*	'Louise'

ダ	*da*	
デ	*de*	
ド	*do*	

Examples:

Places:

a. カナダ	*Kanada*	'Canada'
b. フロリダ	*Hurorida*	'Florida'
c. アムステルダム	*Amusuterudamu*	'Amsterdam'
d. デリー	*Derii*	'Delhi'
e. デンマーク	*Deñmaaku*	'Denmark'
f. ロンドン	*Roñdoñ*	'London'

People:

g. ダン	*Dañ*	'Dan'
h. アイーダ	*Aiida*	'Ida'
i. アダム	*Adamu*	'Adam'
j. ダイアナ	*Daiana*	'Diana'
k. ダニエル	*Danieru*	'Daniel'
l. ダグラス	*Dagurasu*	'Douglas'
m. デニス	*Denisu*	'Dennis'
n. デーナ	*Deena*	'Dana'
o. ドーリス	*Doorisu*	'Doris'
p. ドロシー	*Dorosii*	'Dorothy'

Just as the mora /to/ frequently occurs in the conversion of /t/ from English to Japanese (example: ケート *Keeto* 'Kate'), /do/ is the frequent conversion of English /d/.

CONVERSION RULE 11:
When converting a sequence that contains /do/ back to English, try omitting the /o/.

Examples:
Places:

a. シドニー	*Sidonii*	'Sydney'
b. アイスランド	*Aisurañdo*	'Iceland'
c. アイルランド	*Airurañdo*	'Ireland
d. グリーンランド	*Guriinrañdo*	'Greenland'
e. ロングアイランド	*Ronguairañdo*	'Long Island'

People:

f. ロイド	*Roido*	'Lloyd'
g. エドワード	*Edowaado*	'Edward'
h. ドナルド	*Donarudo*	'Donald'
i. ハロルド	*Harorudo*	'Harold'

バ   ba

ブ   bu

ベ   be

Examples:
Places:

a. バリ	*Bari*	'Bali'

b. バハマ	*Bahama*	'[the] Bahama[s]'
c. ダブリン	*Daburiñ*	'Dublin'
d. ブラジル	*Buraziru*	'Brazil'
e. シベリア	*Siberia*	'Siberia;
f. ベルリン	*Beruriñ*	'Berlin'
g. ベルグラード	*Beruguraado*	'Belgrade'

People:

h. バーバラ	*Baabara*	'Barbara'
i. ロバート	*Robaato*	'Robert'
j. アルバート	*Arubaato*	'Albert'
k. バーナード	*Baanaado*	'Bernard'
l. ブレンダ	*Bureñda*	'Brenda'
m. ブライアン	*Buraiañ*	'Brian'
n. ブルース	*Buruusu*	'Bruce'
o. ベン	*Beñ*	'Ben'
p. イザベル	*Izaberu*	'Isabel'
q. エリザベス	*Erizabesu*	'Elizabeth'

The Japanese sound system includes no /v/ sound. For converting occurrences of /v/ in foreign languages, Japanese has traditionally used mora beginning with /b/.

CONVERSION RULE 12:

When converting a Japanese sequence that contains a mora beginning with /b/ back to its original English, try /v/ as well as /b/.

Examples:
Places:

r. ベトナム	*Betonamu*	'Vietnam'
s. ラスベガス	*Rasubegasu*	'Las Vegas'
t. バンクーバー	*Bankuubaa*	'Vancouver'

People:

u. イブ	*Ibu*	'Eve'

v. エバ	*Eba*	'Eva'
w. バレリー	*Varerii*	'Valerie'
x. オリバー	*Oribaa*	'Oliver'
y. ベバリー	*Bebarii*	'Beverly'
z. バージニア	*Baazinia*	'Virginia'

MARU

The addition of a small circle (*maru*) to any *kana* mora that begins with /h/ changes the value to the corresponding mora that begins with /p/. Compare: ハイ *hai* 'high' and パイ *pai* 'pie'

The following are *katakana* symbols that we can recognize immediately:

パ   *pa*

プ   *pu*

ペ   *pe*

Examples:
Places:

a. パリ	*Pari*	'Paris' (from French)
b. パナマ	*Panama*	'Panama'
c. エジプト	*Eziputo*	'Egypt'
d. アルプス	*Arupusu*	'Alps'
e. ペルー	*Peruu*	'Peru'
f. スペイン	*Supeiñ*	'Spain'

People:

| g. パメラ | *Pamera* | 'Pamela' |

h. ペリー	*Perii*	'Perry'	
i. ペギー	*Pegii*	'Peggy'	
j. プリシラ	*Purisira*	'Priscilla'	

REVIEW

REVIEW 2: Read the following borrowings related to food. Can you read them rapidly, without hesitation???

a. パン _____   b. バター _____

c. マーガリン _____   d. バナナ _____

e. オレンジ _____   f. ストロベリー _____

g. パイ _____   h. プリン _____

i. エクレア _____

j. バニラ・アイスクリーム _____

k. バナナクリームパイ _____

l. トマトスープ _____   m. ハンバーガー _____

n. ハム _____   o. ハムサンド _____

p. サラミ _____   q. パスタ _____

r. ライス _____

REVIEW 3: Identify the following U.S. presidents. (Read the names in Japanese before giving the English equivalents.)

a. ジミー・カーター _____

b. ハーバート・フーバー _____

c. ロナルド・レーガン _____

d. フランクリン・ルーズベルト _____

e. アブラハム．リンカーン   ＿＿＿＿＿＿＿＿＿＿＿

REVIEW 4: Identify the following items in the accompanying *katakana* list. Write the appropriate letter in the parentheses. Again, read the Japanese before giving the English equivalents.

(1) one sport;   (   )

(2) three beverages;   (   ), (   ), (   )

(3) three accessories;   (   ), (   ), (   )

(4) four vehicles   (   ), (   ), (   ), (   )

(5) four articles of clothing (   ), (   ), (   ), (   )

a. タクシー	b. ベルト	c. ミルク
d. スクーター	e. ブレザー	f. ワイン
g. トラクター	h. レスリング	i. スカート
j. スカーフ	k. サングラス	l. ジープ
m. ベスト	n. カクテル	o. ジーンズ

Again, note particularly carefully the *katakana* symbols that resemble each other. It is essential to be able to distinguish them correctly:

フ and ラ and ワ;   ク and タ;   レ and ル;

ノ and メ and ナ;   ア and マ and ム

SUMMARY

The following *katakana* chart incorporates the symbols introduced in Lessons 1 and 2. If you have forgotten any of them, go back to the section where they were introduced and review them thoroughly.

ン ñ	ワ wa	ラ ra	ya	マ ma	ハ ha	ナ na	タ ta	サ sa	カ ka	ア a
		リ ri		ミ mi	hi	ニ ni	ti	シ si	ki	イ i
		ル ru	yu	ム mu	フ hu	nu	tu	ス su	ク ku	u
		レ re		メ me	ヘ he	ne	テ te	se	ケ ke	エ e
		ロ ro	yo	mo	ho	ノ no	ト to	so	ko	オ o

KATAKANA WRITING PRACTICE

	1	2	
wa	イ	ワ	
ha	ノ	ハ	
ra	ー	ラ	
ka	フ	カ	

	1	2	3
me	ノ	メ	
ta	ノ	ク	タ

	1		
hu	フ		
no	ノ		

	1	2	3
o	ー	十	オ

	1	2	3
mi	ー	ニ	三

ANSWER KEY

REVIEW 1:

a, *Rima* 'Lima'; b. *Rooma* 'Rome'; c. *Niisu* 'Nice'; d.*Suisu* 'Switzerland'; e. *Rosia* 'Russia'; f. *Siria* 'Syria' (as a personal name this represents 'Celia'); g. *Siatoru* 'Seattle'; h. *Mareesia* 'Malaysia'; i.*Ruumania* 'Rumania'

REVIEW 2:

a. *pañ* 'bread'(from Portugese); b. *bata* 'butter'; c. *maagarin* 'margarine'; d. *banana* 'banana'; e. *oreñzi* 'orange'; f. *sutorooberii* 'strawberry'; g. *pai* 'pie'; h. *puriñ* 'pudding'; i. *ekurea* 'eclair'; j. *banira aisukuriimu* 'vanilla ice cream'; k. *bananakuriimupai* 'banana cream pie'; l. *tomatosuupu* 'tomato soup'; m. *hañbaagaa* 'hamburger'; n. *hamu* 'ham'; o. *hamusando* 'ham sand(wich)'; p. *sarami* 'salami'; q. *pasuta* 'pasta'; r. *raisu* 'rice' (on a plate)

REVIEW 3:

a. *Zimii Kaataa* 'Jimmy Carter'; b. *Haabaato Huubaa* 'Herbert Hoover'; c. *Ronarudo Reegañ* 'Ronald Reagan'; d. *Hurañkurin Ruuzuberuto* 'Franklin Roosevelt'; *Aburahamu Rinkaañ* 'Abraham Lincoln'

REVIEW 4:

(1). one sport;	h. レスリング *resuriñgu* 'wrestling';
(2). three beverages;	c. ミルク *miruku* 'milk'; n. カクテル *kakuteru* 'cocktail';
(3). three accessories;	b. ベルト *beruto* 'belt'; j. スカーフ *sukaahu* 'scarf'; k. サングラス *sañgurasu* 'sun glass[es]';
(4). four vehicles;	a. タクシー takusii 'taxi'; d. スクーター *sukuutaa* 'scooter'; g. トラクター *torakutaa* 'tractor'; l. ジープ *ziipu* 'jeep';
(5). four articles of clothing:	e. ブレザー *burezaa* 'blazer'; i. スカート *sukaato* 'skirt';m. ベスト *besuto* 'vest'; o. ジーンズ *ziiñzu* 'jeans'

LESSON 3

KATAKANA SYMBOLS (cont.)

We will now continue to add to our inventory of *katakana* symbols.

31. チ   *ti*

The mora /*ti*/ is used to represent both English /chee/ and /tee/, and also /ch/ at the end of words and syllables. Recalling the /t/-column of the mora chart in JSL (page 1), you will remember that the /t/ of /*ti*/ is different from the /t/ of /*ta*/, /*te*/, and /*to*/; it is somewhere between English initial /t/ and /ch/, and not exactly like either.

CONVERSION RULE 13:

For converting an occurrence of /ti/ back to English, try both /tee/ and /chee/ and word- and syllable-final /ch/ as possibilities.

The *katakana* / チ / symbol does not ordinarily occur with *nigori* in representing borrowed words. Again the mora chart is a guide: there is no occurrence of /*di*/ on it. For those other styles of romanization that do use /*di*/, the usual *katakana* equivalent is / ジ /, i.e. / シ *si*/ with *nigori*.

Examples:
Where did you go last year?

a. ハイチ	*Haiti*	'Haiti'
b. カラチ	*Karati*	'Karachi'
c. バチカン	*Batikan*	'Vatican'

Who went with you?

d. アーチ	*Aati*	'Arch'
e. アーチー	*Aatii*	'Archie'

f. マーチン	*Maatiñ*	'Martin'
g. スチーブ	*Sutiibu*	'Steve'
h. クリスチーナ	*Kurisutina*	'Christina'

32. モ   *mo*

モ モ

Examples:
Where are you going on your trip?

a. サモア	*Samoa*	'Samoa'
b. モンタナ	*Montana*	'Montana'
c. モスクワ	*Mosukuwa*	'Moscow' (non-English origin)
d. バーモント	*Baamoñto*	'Vermont'
e. モントリオール	*Moñtoriaaru*	'Montreal'

Who will go with you?

f. モリー	*Moorii*	'Maury'
g. モーリーン	*Mooriiñ*	'Maureen'
h. モリス	*Morisu*	'Morris'
i. モーリス	*Mooriisu*	'Maurice'

33. コ   *ko*

ゴ   *go*

コ ゴ
ゴ ゴ

Examples:
Where were you last year?

a. コスタリカ	*Kosutarika*	'Costa Rica'
b. コペンハーゲン	*Kopeñhageñ*	'Copenhagen'
c. サンフランシスコ	*Sañhurañsisuko*	'San Francisco'
d. シカゴ	*Sikago*	'Chicago'

| e. オレゴン | *Oregoñ* | 'Oregon' |
| f. モンゴル | *Moñgoru* | 'Mongolia' |

Who was with you?

g. コーラ	*Koora*	'Cora'
h. コーリー	*Koorii*	'Cory'
i. コリン	*Koriñ*	'Colin'
j. コーネリアス	*Kooneriasu*	'Cornelius'
k. マーゴ	*Maago*	'Margo'

34. ソ　　*so*

ゾ　　*zo*

We must be sure to note the difference between the symbols / ソ / and / ン /: in / ソ /, the two strokes are lined up horizontally and the long stroke begins at the top; in contrast, the two strokes are lined up vertically in / ン / and the long stroke begins at the bottom.

Examples:

Where are you going?

a. ソマリア	*Somaria*	'Somalia'
b. エルパソ	*Erupaso*	'El Paso'
c. アーカンソー	*Aakañsoo*	'Arkansas'
d. グレート・ソルトレーク	*Gureeto Soruto Reeku*	'Great Salt Lake'
e. アリゾナ	*Arizona*	'Arizona'
f. アマゾン	*Amazoñ*	'Amazon'

With whom?

g. ソウル	*Souru*	'Saul'
h. ソロモン	*Soromoñ*	'Solomon'
i. ゾーイ	*Zooi*	'Zoe'

35. ヒ   *hi*

ビ   *bi*

ピ   *pi*

Examples:

What is that person's name?

a. ヒルダ	*Hiruda*	'Hilda'
b. ヒラリー	*Hirarii*	'Hillary'
c. ビル	*Biru*	'Bill'
d. ビリー	*Birii*	'Billie'
e. シルビア	*Sirubia*	'Sylvia'
f. ビビアン	*Bibiañ*	'Vivian'
g. ピート	*Piito*	'Pete'
h. ピーター	*Piitaa*	'Peter'

Where does s/he come from?

i. タヒチ	*Tahiti*	'Tahiti'
j. リビア	*Ribia*	'Libya'
k. アラビア	*Arabia*	'Arabia'
l. ビルマ	*Biruma*	'Burma'
m. コロンビア	*Koroñbia*	'Columbia'

****

20-SECOND REVIEW: (What is your favorite color?)

a. ブルー	b. ピンク	c. グレー
d. グリーン	e. オリーブ	f. ラベンダー

****

36. キ   *ki*

ギ   *gi*

Examples:
Who is that?

| a. キンバリー | *Kiñbarii* | 'Kimberly' |
| b. ギルバート | *Girubaato* | 'Gilbert' |

Where is s/he going?

c. ワイキキ	*Waikiki*	'Waikiki'
d. ヘルシンキ	*Herusiñki*	'Helsinki'
e. パキスタン	*Pakisutañ*	'Pakistan'
f. イギリス	*Igirisu*	'England' (not a direct conversion)

English /-x/ usually transfers into Japanese as /-*kus*/, particularly in word-final positionor or before a /u/ or /o/ vowel (example: ニクソン *Nikusoñ* 'Nixon'). However, before other vowels, it is often (not always!) converted to /*kis*-/ (examples: テキサス *Tekisasu* 'Texas'; メキシコ *Mekisiko* 'Mexico'.

CONVERSION RULE 14:
Occurrences of both /*kus*-/ and /*kis*-/ may represent conversions of English /x/.

37. ツ   *tu*

We must be able to distinguish the two symbols / ツ / and / シ /: the three strokes of / ツ / are lined up horizontally, with the long stroke beginning at the top of the character. In contrast, the three strokes of / シ / are lined up vertically, with the long stroke beginning at the bottom of the character.

In Japanese, when /t/ is followed by the /u/ vowel, the combination automatically acquires a sound sequence that resembles English /tsu/; there is no mora in Japanese which is pronounced /tu/. It is not surprising, then, that /tu/ becomes the conversion of both /tu/ and /tsu/, with the former much more common. Note: ワ ン, ツ ー, ス リ ー 、 *wan, tuu, surii*, '1,2,3'; ツ ー・ツ ー・ツ ー *tuu tuu tuu* '2 to 2' (telling time in converted English); ツ ナ *tuna* 'tuna'

CONVERSION RULE 15:
An occurrence of /tu/ in Japanese may represent English /tsu/ or, more commonly, /tu/.

Remember! The /u/ vowel, regularly added when borrowing English consonants that end syllables or words or are followed by consonants other than /n/, is usually replaced by the /o/ vowel when the consonant is /t/. Why? Because of the special value of /tu/.

Examples:
Places:

a. ツ ー ル	*Tuuru*	'Tours' (borrowed from French)'
b. ツ ー ロ ン	*Tuuroň*	'Toulon'
c. ド イ ツ	*Doitu*	'Germany' (based on German)

Katakana / ツ /, like / チ /, does not occur with nigori in borrowed words. The mora chart, again, is a guide: there is no /du/ in the /d/- column. For those other systems of romanization that do include a /du/ mora, the *katakana* spelling is / ズ /, i.e., /su/ with *nigori*.

LONG CONSONANTS

The most common use of *katakana* /tu/ is in the writing of long consonants, i.e., those that we regularly represent in romanization with a double consonant. Compare the following items:

(a) ルーク 'Luke'   (b) ルック 'look'

Example (a) has a long vowel, indicated by a double vowel in romanization and the special symbol for vowel lengthening in *katakana*. In (b), the long consonant, indicated in romanization by a double consonant, is represented by *katakana* / ッ / (smaller and lower in horizontal writing, and smaller and to the right in vertical writing) followed by the *katakana* symbol whose initial consonant is the one being lengthened. Even though the / ッ / has reduced size, it is assigned the space given to a full-sized symbol. In handwriting, it is written off-center, slightly closer to the symbol with which it is linked i.e., the one that follows).

This use of / ッ / never occurs at the beginning of a word. However, we occasionally find a reduced / ッ / in final position as an indication of a glottal stop (= a sharp catch in the throat). Thus,   ア   ッ is equivalent to the exclamation 'a!'. We represent this in romanization as *a(tu)*.

Traditionally the only consonants that were ever lengthened -- other than those involving /n̄/[1] -- were /k/, /s/, /t/, and /p/. However, in words recently borrowed into Japanese and written with the *katakana* symbols, we often find reduced / ッ / also in the representation of /-gg-/, /-zz-/, /-dd-/ and /-bb-/. This latter group is representative of a more innovative variety of Japanese. For example, English 'bed' has been borrowed into Japanese both as ベット *betto* and ベッド *beddo*, the first being traditional and the second innovative.

A long /-kk-/, /-ss-/, /-ss-/, or /-pp-/ often occurs in loanwords when the corresponding consonant in English follows a simple vowel (often, but by no

[1]. The combination /-n + m-/ results in a long /m/, /-n + n-/ a long /n/.

means always, at the end of a word) as opposed to a long vowel or diphthong (= two or more vowel qualities within one syllable, as in 'late'), which is followed by a short (= single) consonant. The simple vowels are represented as short vowels in Japanese whereas the long vowels or diphthongs are represented as long vowels or vowel sequences. Compare:

a. スモック *sumokku* 'smock'　　　　and　b. スモーク *sumooku* 'smoke'

c. ヒット *hitto* 'hit'　　　　　　　　and　d. ヒート hiito 'heat'

e. キップ Kippu 'Kip'　　　　　　　　and　f. キープ kiipu 'keep'

In each case we have a /short vowel + long consonant/ on the left and a /long vowel + short consonant/ on the right.

Double-/k/ Combinations:

-ッカ	-*kka*	ッガ	-*gga*
-ッキ	-*kki*	-ッギ	-*ggi*
-ック	-*kku*	-ッグ	-*ggu*
-ッケ	-*kke*	-ッゲ	-*gge*
-ッコ	-*kko*	-ッゴ	-*ggo*

Examples:

Where did you go?

a. メッカ	*Mekka*	'Mecca'
b. ケンタッキー	*Keñtakki*	'Kentucky'
c. ブルックリン	*Burukkuriñ*	'Brooklyn'
d. ストックホルム	*Sutokkuhorumu*	'Stockholm'
e. モロッコ	*Morokko*	'Morocco'

Who went with you?

f. レベッカ	*Rebekka*	'Rebecca'
g. マック	*Makku*	'Mack'
h. リック	*Rikku*	'Rick'
i. ニック	*Nikku*	'Nick'
j. パトリック	*Patorikku*	'Patrick'
k. ドミニック	*Dominikku*	'Dominick'

l. クレッグ   *Kureggu*   'Craig'

Double-/s/ Combinations

-ッサ	-ssa	-ッザ	-zza
-ッシ	-ssi	-ッジ	-zzi
-ッス	-ssu	-ッズ	-zzu
	(-sse		-zze)[2]
-ッソ	-sso	-ッゾ	-zzo

Examples:
Where is she?

a. オデッサ   *Odessa*   'Odessa'
b. ケンブリッジ   *Keñburizzi*   'Cambridge'
c. ブルックリン・ブリッジ   *Burukkuriñ Burizzi*   'Brooklyn Bridge'

Who is she?

d. メリッサ   *Merissa*   'Melissa'
e. マッジ   *Mazzi*   'Madge'
f. ミッジ   *Mizzi*   'Midge'

Double-/t/ Combinations

-ッタ	-tta	ッダ	-dda
-ッチ	-tti		
-ッツ	-ttu		
-ッテ	-tte	ッデ	-dde
--ット	-tto	ッド	-ddo

Examples:
Where are you from?

a. マンハッタン   *Mañhattañ*   'Manhattan'
b. カルカッタ   *Karukatta*   'Calcutta'
c. サンモリッツ   *Sañmorittu*   'San Moritz'

---

[2].This combination cannot be practiced until the *katakana* symbol for /se/ is introduced.

d. ピッツバーグ	*Pittubaagu*	'Pittsburgh'
e. ロッテルダム	*Rotterudamu*	'Rotterdam'
f. チベット	*Tibetto*	'Tibet'
g. スコットランド	*Sukottorañdo*	'Scotland'
h. バグダッド	*Bagudaddo*	'Baghdad'

What is your first name?

i. パット	*Patto*	'Pat'
j. スコット	Sukotto 'Scott'	
k. エリオット	*Eriotto*	'Elliot'
l. トッド	*Toddo*	'Todd'
m. バッド	*Baddo*	'Bud'

Double-/p/ Combinations

-ッパ	*-ppa*		-ッバ	*-bba*
-ッピ	*-ppi*		-ッビ	*-bbi*
-ップ	*-ppu*		-ッブ	*-bbu*
-ッペ	*-ppe*		-ッベ	*-bbe*
	(*-ppo*			*-bbo*)[3]

Examples:

Where are you calling from?

a. ミシシーピ	*Misisippi*	'Mississippi'

Who is with you?

b. キップ	*Kippu*	'Kip';

A REMINDER! *Katakana* / ッ / is never used in representing the lengthening of /*m-*/ and /*n-*/. Instead we find /-*nm-*/ and /-*nn-*/.

Special Combinations

Reduced /*tu*/ may also be used in long consonants, followed by a mora with initial /*h-*/.

---

3. This combination cannot be practiced until the katakana symbol for /ho/ is introduced.

CONVERSION RULE 16:

Again with / ッ/ representing the lengthening of a following consonant, the combination /- ッ フ -hhu/ is used as a conversion of English long /f/, and /-ahha/, /-ihhi/, /-ehhe/ and /-ohho/ approximate the kind of final sounds that occur in German /ach/, /ich/, /ech/ and /och/. Note that in examples of these latter combinations, all borrowed from languages other than English, the vowel following the /-hh-/ in Japanese, which is not present in the original, is the same as the vowel preceding it.

Examples:
What is his name?

a. ゴッホ	*gohho*	'Gogh (from Dutch)'
b. バッハ	*Bahha*	'Bach'(from German)
c. ハインリッヒ	*Haiñrihhi*	'Heinrich' (from German)

****

REVIEW

REVIEW 1. Can you read and identify the following words rapidly and without hesitation? All are related to food and drink. Note in particular examples of the Conversion Rules.

a. レモン	_____	b. パイナップル	_____
c. チキン	_____	d. ロースト・チキン	_____
e. ミートソース	_____	f. ピザ	_____
g. ピラフ	_____	h. チーズ	_____
i. スイスチーズ	_____	j. ブルーチーズ	_____
k. チーズケーキ	_____	l. アップルパイ	_____
m. ドーナツ	_____	n. クッキー	_____
o. ビスケット	_____	p. ジナモン	_____

q. ソーダ _____   r. コカコーラ _____

s. ペプシコーラ _____   t. ビール _____

u. ココア _____

****

KATAKANA SYMBOLS (cont.)

38. ユ   *yu*   ユ ユ

Examples:
Where are you from?

a. ユタ   *Yuta* 'Utah'

b. ユー・エス・エー   *Yuu esu ee* 'U.S.A.'

c. ユナイテッド・ステーツ・オブ・アメリカ   *Yunaiteddo suteetu obu amerika*
                                        'United States of America'

d. ユーゴスラビア   *Yuugosurabia*   'Yugoslavia'

What is your first name?

e. ユージンン   *Yuuziñ*   'Eugene'

f. ユージニア   *Yuuzinia*   'Eugenia'

g. ユーニス   *Yuunisu*   'Eunice'

39. ヤ   *ya*   ヤ ヤ

Examples:
Where?

a. マラヤ   *Maraya*   'Malaya'

b. ヒマラヤ   *Himaraya*   'Himalaya [mountains]'

40. ヨ   *yo*   ヨ ヨ

Examples;

What place is this? (looking at a map)

a. ヨーク   *Yooku*   'York'

b. リヨン   *Riyoñ*   'Lyon'

MORA CONSISTING OF /CONSONANT + /Y/ + VOWEL/

Actually, the most common occurrences of /ya/, /yu/, and /yo/ are within special combinations. Examine the following:

キャ   ギュ   ショ   チャ   ビュ   ピョ

The first *katakana* symbol in each example represents a /consonant + *i*/, and the second, /y + a vowel/. (The only vowels possible are /a/, /u/, and /o/. [See the mora chart on Page 1, *JSL:PART 1*]) This second symbol reminds us of the initial /TU/ in long consonants: assigned a full space but smaller and lower in horizontal writing and smaller and further right in vertical writing; in handwriting it is slightly closer to the symbol it is connected with, in this case the symbol that precedes. These combinations represent *single* mora, romanized as /consonant + *y* + vowel/.

Thus, / ビ ヤ/ is the two-mora sequence /biya/, but / ビ ャ/ is the single mora /bya/. Note that only in such examples is a single mora NOT represented by a single symbol in the Japanese *kana* system.

SUMMARY OF /CONSONANT + Y + VOWEL/ MORA

キャ	*-kya*	シャ	*-sya*	チャ	*-tya*	ニャ	*-nya*
キュ	*-kyu*	シュ	*-syu*	チュ	*-tyu*	ニュ	*-nyu*
キョ	*-kyo*	ショ	*-syo*	チョ	*-tyo*	ニョ	*-nyo*
ギャ	*-gya*	ジャ	*-zya*				
ギュ	*-gyu*	ジュ	*-zyu*				

ギョ	-gyo	ジョ	-zyo				
		ヒャ	-hya	ミャ	-mya	リャ	-rya
		ヒュ	-hyu	ミュ	-myu	リュ	-ryu
		ヒョ	-hyo	ミョ	-myu	リョ	-ryo
ビャ	-bya	ピャ	-pya				
ビュ	byu	ピュ	-pyu				
ビョ	-byo	ピョ	-pyo				

An English word beginning with the /ca/ of 'cab' borrowed into Japanese may have as its initial mora /kya/ instead of /ka/. This reflects an attempt to approximate the difference in pronunciation between this /ca/ and the /ca/ of 'calm', which is always converted as /ka/. Thus we find both *Kyasarin* and *Kasarin* as transfers of 'Katherine' but only *Kaaru* for 'Karl'. Similarly, we find the /ga/ of 'gap' converted as *gyappu*, but only *gaado* for 'guard.'

CONVERSION RULE 17:
Both /ka/ and /kya/ are conversions for English /ca/ or /ka/, and /ga/ and /gya/ for English /ga/.

The existence of these /consonant + *y* + vowel/ mora in Japanese means that conversion from English can distinguish between the initial sounds of pairs like 'socks' (ソックス *sokkusu*) and 'shocks' (ショックス *syokkusu*). It is when we deal with the /i/ vowel that conversions become ambiguous: we have only /si/, /ti/, and /zi/, each of which must represent multiple conversions from English in traditional Japanese writing (cf. the Conversion Rules under each of these katakana symbols).

When the vowel of the /consonant + *y* + vowel/ is lengthened, the symbol indicating length is written in line with the symbols of regular size. Thus:

ニュー   *nyuu*   'new'[4]

The /consonant + *y* + vowel/ mora may be immediately preceded or followed by /ッ/, indicating consonant lengthening.

Thus:

| マッシュルーム | *massyuruumu* | 'mushroom' |
| ショッピングバッグ | *syoppiñgubaggu* | 'shopping bag' |

Examples of /consonant + *y* + vowel/:
Where were you last year:

a. キャンベラ	*Kyañbera*	'Canberra'
b. キューバ	*Kyuuba*	'Cuba'
c. シャンハイ	*Syañhai*	'Shanghai'
d. ジャカルタ	*Zyakaruta*	'Jakarta'
e. ジョージア	*Zyoozia*	'Georgia'
f. チャールストン	*Tyaarusuton*	'Charleston
g. ニューヨーク	*Nyuuyooku*	'New York'
h. ニュージーランド	*Nyuuziirando*	'New Zealand'
i. ヒューロン	*Hyuuroñ*	'Huron'
j. バミューダ	*Bamyuuda*	'Bermuda'

Who was with you?

k. キャシー	*Kyasii*	'Kathie'
l. キャサリン	*Kyasariñ*	'Katharine'
m. シャーリー	*Syaarii*	'Shirley'
n. ロジャー	*Rozyaa*	'Roger'
o. ジョー	*Zyoo*	'Joe'
p. ジョン	*Zyoñ*	'John'
q. ジョーン	*Zyooñ*	'Joan'
r. ジューン	*Zyuuñ*	'June'
s. ジョージ	*Zyoozi*	'George'

4.This is typical of many examples of /consonant + *y* + vowel/ which convert a less commonly heard pronunciation of American English. This represents /nyu/ rather than the more frequently heard /nu/.

t. チャールス	*Tyaarusu*	'Charles'
u. リチャード	*Rityaado*	'Richard'
v. ソーニャ	*Soonya*	'Sonya'
w. ヒュー	*Hyuu*	'Hugh'
x. ヒューゴー	*Hyuugo*	'Hugo'
y. ヒューバート	*Hyuubaato*	'Hubert'
z. サミュエル	*Samyueru*	'Samuel'

REVIEW

REVIEW 2:

A. Identify the following sports, first reading the katakana accurately, carefully retaining long vowels and long consonants whenever they occur:

a. ゴルフ _____   b. ジョギング _____

c. フットボール _____   d. サッカー _____

e. ホッケー _____   f. ランニング _____

g. バスケットボール _____

h. ボーリング _____

i. バレーボール _____   j. レスリング _____

k. ベースボール _____   l. テニス _____

B. With which sports are the following associated?

a. タッチダウン _____   b. ピッチャー _____

c. リレー _____   d. シュート _____

e. サーブ _____   f. キックオフ _____

g. ミット _____   h. キャッチャー _____

i. パー _____   j. ゴールキーパー _____

REVIEW 3: Identify the following U.S. presidents:

a. ハリー・トルーマン   _____

b. ジョージ・ワシントン   _____

c. ジョン・アダムス   _____

d. ベンジャミン・ハリソン   _____

e. カルビン・クーリッジ   _____

f. リンドン・ジョンソン   _____

g. ジョージ・ブッシュ   _____

h. アブラハム・リンカーン   _____

i. リチャード・ニクソン   _____

REVIEW 4: Match the items in the following katakana list with: (1) a statesman; (2) a composer; (3) two articles of clothing; (4) two pizza toppings; (5) two kinds of ice cream; (6) a green vegetable; (7) a kind of hamburger; (8) two nicknames; (9) a beverage; (10) a dessert

a. チョコレート   b. チャーリー   c. ジャケット

d. ブロッコリ   e. メープルナッツ   f. ビッグマック

g. チャーチル   h. アンチョビ   i. ベートーベン

j. ソックス   k. パイナップル・パイ   l. マーガレット

m. オレンジジュース   n. マッシュルーム

(1) a statesman   _____

(2) a composer   _____

(3) two articles of clothing   _____   _____

(4) two pizza toppings   _____   _____

(5) two kinds of ice cream   _____   _____

(6) a green vegetable   _____

(7) a kind of hamburger   _____

(8) two nicknames   _____   _____

(9) a beverage   _____

(10) a dessert   _____

SUMMARY

We now add the symbols learned in Lesson 3 to our table of *gozyuuon*.

ン ñ	ワ wa	ラ ra	ヤ ya	マ ma	ハ ha	ナ na	タ ta	サ sa	カ ka	ア a
		リ ri		ミ mi	ヒ hi	ニ ni	チ ti	シ si	キ ki	イ i
		ル ru	ユ yu	ム mu	フ hu	nu	ツ tu	ス su	ク ku	u
		レ re		メ me	ヘ he	ne	テ te	se	ケ ke	エ e
		ロ ro	ヨ yo	モ mo	ho	ノ no	ト to	ソ so	コ ko	オ o

KATAKANA WRITING PRACTICE

	1	2	3
ti	ノ	ニ	チ
mo	一	ニ	モ
ko	フ	コ	
so	丶	ソ	
hi	一	ヒ	
ki	一	ニ	キ
tu	丶	リ	ツ
small tu	丶	リ	ツ
yu	フ	ユ	

	1	2	
ya	フ	ヤ	
yo	フ	ヲ	ヨ

ANSWER KEY

20-SECONDREVIEW:
a. *buruu* 'blue'; b.*piñku* 'pink'; c.*guree* 'gray'; d. *guriiñ* 'green'; e.*oriibu*'olive'; f.*rabeñdaa* 'lavender'

REVIEW 1:
a. *remoñ* 'lemon'; b. *painappuru* 'pinapple'; c. *tikiñ* 'chicken'; d. *roosutotikiñ* 'roast chicken'; e. *miitosoosu* 'meat sauce'; f. *piza* 'pizza'; g. *pirahu* 'pilaf'; h. *tiizu* 'cheese'; i. *suisutiizu* 'Swiss cheese'; j. *buruutiizu* 'blue cheese'; k. *tiizukeeki* 'cheesecake'; l. *appurupai* 'apple pie'; m. *doonatu* 'doughnut(s)'; n. *kukkii* 'cookie'; o. *bisuketto* 'biscuit'; p. *sinamoñ* 'cinnamon'; q. *sooda* 'soda'; r. *Kokakoora* 'Coca Cola'; s. *Pepusiikoora* 'Pepsi Cola'; t. *biiru* 'beer'; u. *kokoa* 'cocoa'

REVIEW 2:
A. a. *goruhu* 'golf'; b. *zyogiñgu* 'jogging'; c. *huttobooru* 'football'; d. *sakkaa* 'soccer'; e. *hokkee* 'hockey'; f. *rañniñgu* 'running'; g. *basukettobooru* 'basketball'; h. *booriñgu* 'bowling'; i. *bareebooru* 'volley ball'; j. *resuriñgu* 'wrestling'; k. *beesubooru* 'baseball'; l. *tenisu* 'tennis'

B. a. *tattidauñ* 'touchdown' -- フットボール; b. *pittyaa* 'pitcher' -- ベースボール; c. *riree* 'relay'-- ランニング; d. *syuuto* 'shoot' -- バスケットボール; e. *saabu* 'serve' -- バレーボール; f. *kikkuofu* 'kickoff' -- フットボール; g. *mitto* 'mitt' -- ベースボール; h. *kyattyaa* 'catcher' -- ベースボール; i. *paa* 'par' -- ゴルフ; j. *goorukiipaa* 'goalkeeper' -- サッカー, ホッケー

REVIEW 3:
a. *Harii Toruumañ* 'Harry Truman'; b. *Zyoozi Wasintoñ* 'George Washington'; c. *Zyon Adamusu* 'John Adams'; d. *Beñzyamin Harisoñ* 'Benjamin Harrison'; e. *Karubiñ Kuurizzi* 'Calvin Coolidge'; f. *Riñdon Zyonsoñ* 'Lyndon Johnson'; g. *Zyoozi Bussyu* 'George Bush'; h. *Aburahamu Rinkaañ* 'Abraham Lincoln'; i. *Rityaado Nikusoñ* 'Richard Nixon'

REVIEW 4:

(1) a statesman	g. チャーチル *Tyaatiru* 'Churchill'
(2) a composer	i. ベートーベン *Beetobeñ* 'Beethoven'
(3) two articles of clothing	c. ジャケット *zyaketto* 'jacket'; j. ソックス *sokkusu* 'socks'
(4) two pizza toppings	h. アンチョビ *añtyobi* 'anchovy'; n. マッシュルーム *massyuruumu* 'mushroom'
(5) two kinds of ice cream	a. チョコレート *tyokoreeto* 'chocolate'; e. メープルナッツ *meepurunattu* 'maple nut'
(6) a green vegetable	d. ブロッコリ *burokkorii* 'broccoli'

(7) a kind of hamburger

f. ビッグマック *biggumakku* 'Big Mac'

(8) two given names

b. チャーリー *Tyaarii* 'Charlie'; l. マーガレット *Maagarette* 'Margaret'

(9) a beverage

m. オレンジジュース *orenzizyuusu* 'orange juice'

(10) a dessert

k. パイナップル・パイ *painappurupai* 'pineapple pie'

LESSON 4

KATAKANA SYMBOLS (cont.)

First, we will learn the 5 remaining katakana symbols in common use.

41. ホ   *ho*

    ボ   *bo*

    ポ   *po*

Remember that *katakana* syllables beginning with /b/ may represent English sequences beginning with /v/.

Examples:
Where did you go?

a. ホノルル	*Honoruru*	'Honolulu'
b. ホンコン	*Hoñkoñ*	'Hongkong'
c. オクラホマ	*Okurahoma*	'Oklahoma'
d. ボスニア	*Bosunia*	'Bosnia'
e. リスボン	*Risuboñ*	'Lisbon'
f. ポーランド	*Poorañdo*	'Poland'
g. ポートランド	*Pootorañdo*	
or		
ポルトランド	*Porutorañdo*	'Portland'
h. ポルトガル	*Porutogaru*	Portugal'

Who went with you?

i. ホレース	*Horeesu*	'Horace'
j. ホリー	*Horii*	'Holly'

k. デボラ	*Debora*	'Deborah'
l. ボーン	*Booñ*	'Vaughn'
m. ポリー	*Porii*	'Polly'
n. ポール	*Pooru*	'Paul'
o. ポーラ	*Poora*	'Paula'
p. ポーリーン	*Pooriiñ*	'Pauline'

42. セ   *se*   セ セ

ゼ   *ze*   ゼ ゼ

Examples:
Where are you going?

a. セントルイス	*Señtoruisu*	'St. Louis'
b. セントポール	*Señtopooru*	'St. Paul'
c. セントローレンス	*Señtorooreñsu*	'St. Lawrence'
d. マサチューセッツ	*Masatyuusetu*	'Massachusetts'

Who is going with you?

e. セルマ	*Seruma*	'Selma'
f. エセル	*Eseru*	'Ethel'
g. ゼルダ	*Zeruda*	'Zelda'
h. ヘーゼル	*Heezeru*	'Hazel'
g. セーラ	*Seera*	'Sarah'

Katakana セ has also traditionally been used as a conversion for English /che/ as in 'cello' (*katakana* セロ), and katakana ゼ for English /je/ as in 'jelly' (*katakana* ゼリー).

CONVERSION RULE 18:
For occurrences of katakana / セ/, try English /che/ as well as /se/ as conversions; and for /ゼ/, try /je/ as well as /ze/.

Example:
Where?

i. ロスアンゼルス	*Rosuañzerusu*	'Los Angeles'

Who?

j. アンゼラ	*Añzera*	'Angela'
k. エンゼル	*Eñzeru*	'Angel'

43. ウ   *u*

Katakana ウ represents /u/ when it occurs as a mora by itself (but not as lengthening of a preceding vowel).

Examples:
Where did you go?

a. ウルグアイ	*Uruguai*	'Uruguay'
b. サウスアメリカ	*Sausuamerika*	'South America'
c. サウスダコタ	*Sausudakota*	'South Dakota'
d. サウスカロライナ	*Sausukaroraina*	'South Carolina'
e. サウジアラビア	*Sauziarabia*	'Saudi Arabia'

Who went with you?

f. ウルスラ	*Urusura*	'Ursula'

You will remember that /w/ occurs only before the /a/ vowel in modern Japanese. Thus, we do have a single *katakana* symbol / ワ /, but not one for the other /w + vowel/ combinations. When /w/ occurs before other vowels in English, the Japanese conversion uses /u/ before the appropriate vowel. When that vowel is u, the result is a long (= double *u*), as in *uuru* 'wool'.

CONVERSION RULE 19:
The mora /u/ followed directly by a vowel other than /a/ may represent English /w/.

Examples:
Where?

a. ウエストポイント	*Uesutopoiñto*	'West Point'
b. ウエストバージニア	*Uesutobaazinia*	'West Virginia'

Who?

c. ウイリアム	*Uiriamu*	'William'
d. ウインストン	*Uiñsutoñ*	'Winston'
e. ウインフレッド	*Uiñihureddo*	'Winfred'

44. ネ   *ne*

Examples:
Where does he come from?

a. ネパール	*Nepaaru*	'Nepal'
b. ネバダ	*Nebada*	'Nevada'
c. テネシー	*Tenesii*	'Tennessee'
d. ミネソタ	*Minesota*	'Minnesota'
e. ネブラスカ	*Neburasuka*	'Nebraska'
f. ゼネガル	*Senegaru*	'Senegal'
g. インドネシア	*Iñdonesia*	'Indonesia'
h. ネプルス	*Nepurusu*	'Naples'
i. ミネアポリス	*Mineaporisu*	'Mineapolis
j. リオ・デ・ジャネイロ	*Riodezyaneiro*	'Rio de Janeiro'

What is your friend's name?

k. ネーサン	*Neesañ*	'Nathan'
l. ネリー	*Nerii*	'Nellie'
m. ケネス	*Kenesu*	'Kenneth'
n. アグネス	*Agunesu*	'Agnes'

45. ヌ   *nu*

We have learned that the usual conversion for a word-final /ñ/ is the nasal mora / ン /. However, for some words that end in a stressed syllable that has a final /n/, the Japanese conversion ends in /ñnu/. This is particularly common in words borrowed from French.

Examples:
Where did you stay?

a. ローザンヌ   *Roozañnu*   'Lausanne'

Who went with you?

b. ロザンヌ   *Rozañnu*   'Roseanne'

d. マリアンヌ   *Mariañnu*   'Marianne'

****

REVIEW

REVIEW 1: Here are some lists of Japanese loanwords for additional reading practice. Are you beginning to see a word as a single unit instead of proceeding painfully, symbol by symbol?

A. Office-related items:

a. ペン   _____   b. ボールペン   _____

c. テープ   _____   d. セロテープ   _____

e. ネームプレート   _____   f. ブックエンド   _____

g. タイプライター   _____   h. コンピュータ   _____

i. ワー(ド)プロ(セッサ)   _____

j. フロッピー   _____   k. メッセージ   _____

l. アルバイト   _____   m. マネージャー   _____

n. コンサルタント   _____

B. How did you come here?

a. スクーター _____ b. バス _____

c. タクシー _____ d. リムジンバス _____

e. ハイヤー _____ f. スポーツカー _____

g. ヘリコプター _____ h. モノレール _____

i. モーターボート _____ j. カヌー _____

C. Which of the following is your favorite sport?

a. テニス b. ピンポン

c. ゴルフ d. バスケットボール

e. フットボール f. バレーボール

g. サッカー h. セーリング

i. ハイキング j. ソーリング

k. ジョギング l. ランニング

m. サイクリング n. ボーリング

o. スケート p. アイススケート

D. Which of these ice cream flavors do you like best?

a. チョコレートチップ b. モカチップ

c. バニラ d. バナナ

e. ピーチ f. ストロベリー

g. メープル・ウオールナッツ h. ヒスタチオ

****

All the *katakana* symbols in common use have now been introduced. A few more symbols, representing only out-of-date, historical spellings, will be introduced later.

SUMMARY

Our table of *gozyuuon* now looks like this:

ン ń	ワ wa	ラ ra	ヤ ya	マ ma	ハ ha	ナ na	タ ta	サ sa	カ ka	ア a
		リ ri		ミ mi	ヒ hi	ニ ni	チ ti	シ si	キ ki	イ i
		ル ru	ユ yu	ム mu	フ hu	ヌ nu	ツ tu	ス su	ク ku	ウ u
		レ re		メ me	ヘ he	ネ ne	テ te	セ se	ケ ke	エ e
		ロ ro	ヨ yo	モ mo	ホ ho	ノ no	ト to	ソ so	コ ko	オ o

INNOVATIVE PRONUNCIATION

In the more recent borrowing of words into Japanese, some are pronounced with features of innovative pronunciation that are not covered in our traditional chart of 113 mora. In every case, this innovative pronunciation is closer to -- BUT NOT EXACTLY THE SAME AS -- that of the original foreign word. To represent these newer pronunciations, special conventions for the use of *katakana* have been adopted:

1. The combinations /テュ/, /デュ/, /フュ/ reflect the same principle that was described in Lesson 3 in connection with combinations like /チャ/, /ジュ/, and /ヒョ/, i.e., the first symbol in each case keeps only its original consonant

value and loses its vowel value; the second symbol has its usual value. The resulting combination is one single mora, pronounced with one beat. We will represent these innovative mora in romanization with the deleted vowel in parentheses: /t(e)yu/ = the /t/ of /te/ + /yu/, pronounced as a single mora, /d(e)yu/ = the /d/ of /de/ + /yu/ pronounced as a single mora, and /h(u)yu/ = the /h/ of /hu/ + /yu/, again pronounced as a single mora.

Examples:

a. テューバ	*t(e)yuba*	'tuba'
b. エデュケーション	*ed(e)yuukeesyoñ*	'education'
c. フューネラル	*h(u)yuuneraru*	'funeral'

In the traditional variety of Japanese, /チュ/, /ジュ/, and /ヒュ/ occur instead, with different pronunciation. The crucial difference in the writing is whether the initial symbol is traditional /consonant + i/ or innovative /consonant + other vowel/.

2. A vowel symbol written smaller and lower (or further right, in vertical texts) than surrounding symbols also indicates that the preceding symbol has its consonant value only. For example, the combination /フェ/ stands for a single mora consisting of the /h/ of /hu/ + /e/. Again we will represent this in romanization with the deleted vowel in parentheses: /h(u)e/.

This procedure makes it possible to produce mora that are significantly closer to various combinations in foreign languages that do not occur in Japanese at all. For example, only /h/ before /u/ represents a sound in Japanese that is at all close[1] to that of /f/; before other vowels, /h/ has no resemblance to /f/. Thus, in converting English /f/ followed by vowels other than /u/, the /hu/ mora with deleted /u/ followed by a vowel results in a closer approximation of the original than a simple /ha/, /hi/, /he/, or /ho/, as used in traditional spelling:

[1].English /f/ is made with the upper teeth and lower lip, whereas Japanese /h/ is made with the upper lip and lower lip.

フォーク is closer to 'fork' than ホーク; ファックス is closer to 'FAX' than ハックス.

The more commonly occurring *katakana* combinations in this category, followed by their traditional equivalents, are:

ティ	*t(e)i*	チ	*ti*	シェ	*s(i)e*	セ	*se*
ディ	*d(e)i*	ジ	*zi*	ジェ	*z(i)e*	ゼ	*ze*
トゥ	*t(o)u*	ツ	*tu*				
ドゥ	*d(o)u*	ズ	*zu*				
チェ	*t(i)e*	チ	*ti*				

ファ	*h(u)a*	ハ	*ha*
フィ	*h(u)i*	ヒ	*hi*
フェ	*h(u)e*	ヘ	*he*
フォ	*h(u)o*	ホ	*ho*

Examples: (Innovative spelling followed by traditional in parentheses)
Names of people and places:

a. マーティン (マーチン) *Maat(e)iñ (Maatiñ)*   'Martin'
b. ディック (ジック) *D(e)ikku (Zikku)*   'Dick'
c. フェルドナンド (ヘルドナンド)
        H(u)erud(e)inañdo (Heruzinañdo)   'Ferdinand'
d. チェスター (セスター)
        T(i)esutaa (Sesutaa) 'Chester'
e. シェリー (セリー)   *S(i)erii (Serii)*   'Shelley'
f. ジェラルド (ゼラルド)   *Z(i)erarudo (Zerarudo)* 'Gerald'
g. ジェフリー (ゼフリー)   *Z(i)ehurii (Zehurii)*   'Jeffrey'
h. ドゥーク・オブ・エディンバラ (ジューク・オブ・エジンバラ)
        (*D(o)uuku obu   Ed(e)iñbara (Zyuuku obu Eziñbara)*
        'Duke of Edinborough'
i. カートゥーム (カーツーム)
        Kaat(o)uumu (Kaatuumu)   'Khartoum'

j. フィンランド (ヒンランド)

       H(u)iñrañdo (Hiñrañdo)   'Finland'

k. ファーイースト (ハーイースト)

       H(u)aaiisuto (Haaiisuto)   'Far East'

l. ハードフォード (ハードホード)

       Haatoh(u)oodo (Haatohoodo)   'Hartford'

m. フィリピン (ヒリピン)   *H(u)iripiñ (Hiripiñ)*   'Philippine[s]'

n. チェコスロバキア (チコスロバキア)

       T(i)ekosurobakia (Tikosurobakia)   'Czechoslavakia'

3. The mora /wa/ occurs both in native Japanese words and in loanwords, but /w/ does not occur before any vowels other than /a/ in native Japanese words. In loanwords, the conversion for /w + vowels other than a/ in traditional spelling is /ui/, /uu/, /ue/, and /uo/, as was previously pointed out. To represent innovative pronunciation, which retains the foreign /w/ in these combinations, /u/ is followed by the vowels /i/, /e/, and /o/ in reduced form, resulting in single mora. These innovative forms will be represented in romanization as /wi/, /we/, and /wo/. However, the /w + u/ sequence continues to be a long /u/ vowel, as in ウーマン *uuman* 'woman'; there is no special innovative pronunciation or spelling for this combination.

Examples:

Personal names: (Traditional spelling follows the innovative in parentheses)

a. ウィリアム (ウイリアム)   *Wiriamu (Uiriamu)*   'William'

b. ウィンフレッド (ウインフレッド)

       Wiñihureddo (Uiñihureddo)   'Winifred'

c. ウェンディー(ウエンジー)

       Weñd(e)ii (Ueñzii)   'Wendy'

d. ウォルター (ウオルター)

       Worutaa (Uoorutaa)   'Walter'

e. エドウィン (エドウイン)   *Edowiñ (Edouiñ)*   'Edwin'

f. ウドロー・ウィルソン (ウドロー・ウイルソン)

Udoroo Wirusoñ (Udoroo Uirusoñ)   'Woodrow Wilson'

g. ウェスリー（ウエスリー）   *Wesurii (Uesurii)*   'Wesley'

4. The *katakana* combination / ク エ/ occurs in loanwords as a representation of the sound sequence /kwe/, and / ク オ/ as a representation of /kwo/. These combinations will be represented in romanization as /*kwe*/ and /*kwo*/. In traditional spelling, / ク エ/ and / ク オ/ occur instead, indicating the traditional two-mora pronunciation of each sequence.

Example:

ラテン・クォーター（ラテン・クオーター）

　　　　Rateñ kwotaa (Raten kuotaa)   'Latin Quarter'

5. *Katakana* /u + *nigori*/ / ヴ/ is used to represent the innovative pronunciation /v/ in loanwords. It will be romanized as /*v*/. With a following reduced vowel / ア/, / イ/, / エ/, or / オ/, the combination represents /v + that vowel/. Without a following reduced vowel, / ヴ/ represents the mora /vu/ all by itself. In traditional Japanese, *ba, bi, bu, be,* and bo occur instead of these special combinations.

Examples:
People and places: (Traditional spelling follows the innovative in parentheses)

a. ヴァレリー（バレリー）   *Varerii (Barerii)*   'Valerie'

b. ヴィンセント（ビンセント）

　　　　Viñseñto (Biñseñto)   'Vincent'

c. ヴィヴィアン（ビビアン）   *Viviañ (Bibiañ)*   'Vivian'

d. ヴェラ（ベラ）   *Vera (Bera)*   'Vera'

e. ヴェロニカ（ベロニカ）   *Veronika (Beronika)*   'Veronica'

f. キエヴ（キエブ）   *Kievu (Kiebu)*   'Kiev'

g. ヴォルガ（ボルガ）   *Voruga (Boruga)*   'Volga' (river)

h. ヴァンクーヴァー（バンクーバー）

　　　　Vañkuuvaa (Bañkuubaa)   'Vancouver'

6. When katakana / イ/ is followed by the vowel / エ/ in reduced form, it assumes the /y/ value of /ya/, and the combination represents a single mora /ye/, which occurs only in borrowed words. In traditional pronunciation and spelling, a two-mora sequence / イ エ/ or / エ エ/ occurs instead, as has been previously pointed out. Thus: イ エ メ ン *Yemeñ* (for traditional イ エ メ ン *Iemeñ* or エ ー メ ン *Eemeñ*) 'Yemen'

There is no consistency in the use of innovative pronunciations and spellings. In no sense have they completely replaced the traditional: for some items, one or the other style is regularly used, but for others, either style is apt to occur. And it is not unusual to find even single words that contain an example of both styles, in both speaking and writing.

****

REVIEW

REVIEW 2: Can you identify these words of general usage that occur in a wide variety of contexts?

a. チャンス _____ b. アイディア _____

c. システム _____ d. アクセス _____

e. ステータス _____ f. アプローチ _____

g. イデオロギー _____ h. サイドステップ _____

i. ネットワーク _____ j. ライフスタイル _____

k. アイデンティティー _____

l. フロンティア _____ m. インセンティヴ _____

n. ダイナミック _____

****

ABBREVIATED FORMS

There is one type of *katakana* example that the foreigner is usually unable to understand without help from a native speaker or a dictionary: abbreviated forms. English, too, has similar forms: for example, 'hazmats' for 'hazardous materials' represents one type and the entire world of acronyms, another (example: 'WAC' for 'Women's Army Corps'). These are usually incomprehensible unless the shortening has been learned as a separate lexical item or explained. Japanese *katakana* abbreviations present a problem for the foreigner, particularly since they occur so frequently and are entering the language at such a rapid pace. It is easy to see why this phenomenon is so popular in Japanese: so many borrowed words end up having a large number of mora, presenting a strong temptation to make them shorter and simpler. Why struggle with コ ネ ク シ ョ ン *konekusyoñ* 'connection', requiring five beats to pronounce and taking up six boxes on the written page, when コ ネ will do just as well? プ ロ can take care of プロフェッ ショ ナ ル *puroh(e)ssyonaru* 'professional' and プ ロ パ ガ ン ダ *puropaganda* 'propaganda' and more, depending on context, but foreigners will need help until they learn what a particular occurrence stands for. Who, without assistance, could possibly guess the meaning of リ ス ト ラ (from リ ス ト ラ ク チ ャ リ ン グ *risutorakutyuariñgu* 'restructuring')?

The vast majority of Japanese shortenings are the beginning portion of a longer word; only rarely does the end portion become the abbreviation. One example that has been in the language for a long time is ホ ー ム from プ ラ ッ ト ホ ー ム *purattohoomu* 'platform'. (Note the traditional / ホ / instead of innovative / フ ォ /.)

In many cases, the abbreviated form occurs as a word by itself, as in the examples above; in other examples, it becomes part of a compound together with an unabbreviated item: thus, マスコミ, from マス *masu* 'mass' + コミュニケーション *komyuunikeesyoñ* 'communication.'

Examples that are most difficult to understand without help are compounds in which both parts are shortenings: thus, セクハラ from セクシュアル *sekusyuaru* 'sexual' + ハラスメント *harasumeñto* 'harassment.'

Abbreviated forms develop when borrowed items are long, occur frequently, and gain wide recognition. Some become sufficiently entrenched in the language to be accepted as permanent members of the lexicon and listed in dictionaries.

Note the following examples:

a. ワープロ from   ワード・プロセッサー

         waado purosessaa   'word processor'

b. パソコン from   パーソナル・コンピュータ2

         pasonaru koñpyuuta   'personal computer'

c. オフコン from   オフィス・コンピュータ

         oh(u)isu koñpyuuta   'office computer'

d. リモコン from   リモート・コントロール

         rimooto koñtorooru   'remote control'

e. ハンスト from   ハンガー・ストライキ

         hangaa sutoraiki   'hunger strike'

f. クロカン from   クロス・カントリー

         kurosu kañtorii 'cross country'

g. ダンパ from   ダンス・パーティー3

         dañsu paat(e)ii 'dance party'

****

2. Note the automatic difference in pronunciation of /ン *n*/ when it occurs before /*p*/ in コンピュータ and at the end of the word in パソコン.

3. Again note the change in the value of /ン *n*/ in the original and in the abbreviated form.

Reading even the most advanced levels of Japanese means continued contact with *katakana*. Depending on the subject matter, there may be frequent examples -- as when a passage deals with electronics and is filled with loanwords or includes many foreign place or personal names -- or few examples -- as when the passage contains only random borrowings of more general usage, like ケ ー ス バ イ ケ ー ス *keesu bai keesu* 'case-by-case', or ウ ィ ー ク ポ イ ン ト *wiikupointo* 'weak point'. But contact there will be. Comparison of the front pages of Japanese newspapers of today as compared with those of a generation ago shows a striking overall increase in the amount of *katakana*. A student of Japanese is well-advised to master *katakana* thoroughly, in order to be able to handle examples with ease.

Here are some additional lists of *katakana* items for reading practice. Develop reading fluency, remembering to read what is actually represented by the *katakana*; do not slide into the foreign pronunciation of the word that is the basis for the borrowing as soon as it is recognized.

From an automotive magazine:

a. エンジン	*eñziñ*	'engine'
b. ブレーキ	*bureeki*	'brake'
c. ギア	*gia*	'gear'
d. ヒーター	*hiitaa*	'heater'
e. バックミラー	*bakkumiraa*	'back (= rearview) mirror'
f. ヘッドライト	*heddoraito*	'headlight'
g. テールライト	*teeruraito*	'tail-light'
h. タイヤ	*taiya*	'tire'
i. ニヤミス	*niyamisu*	'near miss,' 'close call'
j. フォード	*H(u)oodo*	'Ford'
k. プリモス	*Purimosu*	'Plymouth'
l. シボレー	*Siboree*	'Chevrolet'
m. リンカーン	*Riñkaañ*	'Lincoln'

n. キャディラック	*Kyad(e)irakku*	'Cadillac'
o. ボルボ	*Borubo*	'Volvo'
p. サーブ	*Saabu*	'Saab'
q. フォルクス(ワーゲン)	*H(u)orukusu(wageñ)*	'Volkswagen'
r. ベンツ	*Beñtu*	'[Mercedes] Benz'
s. ロールスロイス	*Roorusuroisu*	'Rolls Royce'
t. ジャガー	*Zyagaa*	'Jaguar'

From a fashion magazine:

a. スーツ	*suutu*	'suit'
b. ベスト	*besuto*	'vest'
c. セーター	*seetaa*	'sweater[4]'
5d. クルーネック・セーター	*kuruuneku seetaa*	'crewneck sweater'
e. ブレザー	*burezaa*	'blazer'
f. ジャツ	*syatu*	'shirt'
g. ワイシャツ	*waisyatu*	'whi[te] [= dress] shirt'
h. ハワイシャツ	*hawaisyatu*	'Hawai[ian] shirt'
i. ショーツ	*syootu*	'shorts'
j. パンツ	*pañtu*	'pants'
k. ウール・パンツ	*uuru pañtu*	'wool pants'
l. ジーンズ	*ziiñzu*	'jeans'
or		
ジーパン	*ziipañ*	'[blue] jea[n] pan[ts]'
or		
ブルージーンズ	*buruuziiñzu*	'bluejeans'
m. レーンコート	*reeñkooto*	'raincoat'
n. ダウン・ジャケット	*dauñ zyaketto*	'down coat'
o. スプリングコート	*supuriñgukooto*	'spring coat'
p. ネクタイ	*nekutai*	'necktie'

4. While almost all *katakana* examples can be understood on the basis of fixed rules, there is the occasional exception. This frequently occurring loanword is such an example.

q. スカーフ   *sukaahu*   'scarf'

r. マフラー   *mahuraa* 'muffler'

s. ベルト   *beruto*   'belt'

t. ソックス   *sokkusu*   'socks'

u. スニーカー   *suniikaa*   'sneaker[s]'

v. ブーツ   *buutu*   'boots'

w. スカート   *sukaato*   'skirt'

x. ブラウス   *burausu*   'blouse'

y. チャケット   *zyaketto*   'jacket'

z. ワンピース   *wañpiisu*   'one-piece [dress]'

a'. ツーピース   *tuupiisu*   'two-piece [dress]'

b'. イブニングドレス   *ibuniñgudoresu*   'evening dress'

c'. ポリエステル・キュロット・スーツ

     poriesuteru kyurottosuutu   'polyester culotte[s] suit'[5]

From a pizza menu:

a. ドミノピザ - **No.1** デリバリーピザチェーン

     Domino piza - No.1 deribariipizat(i)eeñ

     'Domino Pizza - No.1 Delivery Piza Chain'

b. アメリカン・スペシャル   *amerikañ supesyaru*   'American Special'

c. ペパロニ、 オニオン、 ダブルチーズ

     peparoni, onioñ, daburutiizu   'Pepperoni, Onion, Double cheese'

d. ゴールデン・デライト   *gorudeñ deraito*   'Golden Delight'

e. ピーマン、 コーン、 ハム

     piimañ, kooñ, hamu   'Pimien[to], Corn, Ham'

f. イタリアンソーセージ   *itariañsooseezi*   'Italian sausage'

g. エキストラ・チーズ   *ekisutora tiizu*   'Extra cheese'

h. ドミノ・スーパーデラックス

     Domino suupaaderakkusu   'Domino Super Deluxe'

[5].This is typical of many *katakana* fashion items that do not normally occur in English. Some are difficult for the native speaker of English to understand.

i. ペパロニ、マッシュルーム
      peparoni, massyuruumu   'Pepperoni, Mushroom'

j. オニオン、イタリアンソーセージ
      onioň, itariaňsooseezi   'Onion Italian, sausage'

k. ピーマン、ブラックオリーブ
      piimaň, burakkuoriibu   'Pimien[to], Black olive(s)'

l. ハム、ベーコン、エキストラ・チーズ
      hamu, beekoň, ekisutora tiizu   'Ham, Bacon, Extra cheese'

From the description of a baseball game:

a. チーム	*tiimu*	'team'	
b. キャッチャー	*kya*	ttyaa 'catcher'	
c. ピッチャー	*pittyaa*	'pitcher'	
d. バッター	*battaa*	'batter'	
e. ワンボール	*waňbooru*	'ball 1'	
f. ツーボール	*tuubooru*	'ball 2'	
g. スリーボール	*suriibooru*	'ball 3'	
h. アウト	*auto*	'out'	
i. セーフ	*seehu*	'safe'	
j. ストライク	*sutoraiku*	'strike'	
k. スリーストライク	*suriisutoraiku*	'strike 3'	
l. ファースト	*h(u)aasuto*	'first [base]'	
m. セカンド	*sekaňdo*	'second [base]'	
n. サード	*saado*	'third [base]'	
o. ファウル	*h(u)auru*	'foul'	
p. ファンブル	*h(u)aňburu*	'fumble'	
q. ホームラン	*hoomuraň*	'home run'	
r. ファインプレー	*h(u)aiňpuree*	'fine play'	
s. ウォーミングアップ	*woomiňguappu*	'warming up'	
t. バット	*batto*	'bat'	
u. ミット	*mitto*	'mitt'	
v. ユニホーム	*yu*	nihoomu 'uniform'	

When *katakana* occurs as part of a Japanese text, it is usually a text written in *hiragana* and *kanzi*, with unit examples of *katakana* within it. While *katakana* examples frequently occur in isolation, it is most unusual to find a text written entirely or principally in *katakana*. Thus the fluent reader of Japanese is constantly required to switch to *katakana* from other types of script -- without any hesitation or slowing down.

As a substitute for switching among Japanese scripts, the following is a short exercise for practicing reading a few *katakana* examples within English contexts, to test your speed in reading them. Are you able to insert the Japanese in the English sentences that follow without altering your reading pace??? (Of course this works as a true test only the first time the sentences are read.)

1. They have been in this country for all of two years but they are still ホーム シック.

2. His arrival on campus in traditional Japanese-style clothing created a センセーション.

3. Ms. Nakamura, the only woman faculty member at this school, is known as a true フェミニスト, active in the ウーマンリブ movement.

4. The high point of the concert was the playing of the piano コンチェルト.

5. This situation creates a ジレンマ that knows no easy solution.

6. He cannot imagine breakfast without his オートミール.

7. When she orders a hamburger or a hot dog, she immediately asks for ケチャップ.

8. This manuscript is filled with ミスプリント.

9. To have so much bad luck lately makes me think I have a ジンクス.

10. I like books and plays that have a ハッピーエンド.

SUMMARY

The following table indicates the overall order in which the katakana symbols were introduced.

ン 6	ワ 21	ラ 23	ヤ 39	マ 15	ハ 22	ナ 2	タ 26	サ 4	カ 24	ア 7
		リ 3		ミ 30	ヒ 35	ニ 1	チ 31	シ 17	キ 36	イ 16
		ル 14	ユ 38	ム 9	フ 27	ヌ 45	ツ 37	ス 12	ク 13	ウ 43
		レ 18		メ 25	ヘ 19	ネ 44	テ 5	セ 42	ケ 10	エ 20
		ロ 11	ヨ 40	モ 32	ホ 41	ノ 28	ト 8	ソ 34	コ 33	オ 29

KATAKANA WRITING PRACTICE

	1	2	3	4
ho	一	十	オ	ホ
se	一	セ		
u	ヽ	ハ	ウ	
ne	ヽ	ラ	ネ	ネ
nu	フ	ヌ		

ANSWER KEY

REVIEW 1:

A: a. *peñ* 'pen'; b. *boorupeñ* 'ball[point] pen'; c. *teepu* 'tape'; d. *seroteepu* 'cello[phane] tape'; e. *neemupureeto* 'name-plate'; f. *bukkueñdo* 'bookend[s]'; g. *taipuraitaa* 'typewriter'; h. *koñpyuuta* 'computer'; i. *waa(do)puro(sessaa)* 'word processor'; j. *huroppii* 'floppy [disk]'; k. *messeezi* 'message'; l. *arubaito* 'arbeit' (German) (= part-time work[er]); m. *maneezyaa* 'manager'; n. *koñsarutanto* 'consultant'

B: a. *sukuutaa* 'scooter'; b. *basu* 'bus'; c. *takusii* 'taxi'; d. *rimoziñbasu* 'limousine bus'; e. *haiyaa* 'hire[d limo]'; f. *supootukaa* 'sportscar'; g. *herikoputaa* 'helicopter'; h. *monoreeru* 'monorail'; i. *mootaabooto* 'motor boat'; j. *kanuu* 'canoe'

C: a. *tenisu* 'tennis'; b. *piñpoñ* 'ping pong'; c. *goruhu* 'golf'; d. *basukettobooru* 'basketball'; e. *huttobooru* 'football'; f. *bareebooru* 'volley ball'; g. *sokkaa* 'saccer'; h. *seeriñgu* 'sailing'; i. *haikiñgu* 'hiking'; j. *sooriñgu* 'soaring'; k. *zyogiñgu* 'jogging'; l. *rañniñgu* 'running'; m. *saikuriñgu* 'cycling'; n. *booriñgu* 'bowling'; o. *sukeeto* 'skat[ing]'; p. *aisusukeeto* 'ice-skat[ing]'

D: a. *tyokoreetotippu* 'chocolate chip'; b. *mokatipu* 'mocha chip'; c. *banira* 'vanilla'; d. *banana* 'banana'; e. *piiti* 'peach'; f. *sutoroberii* 'strawberry'; g. *meepuru uoorunattu* 'maple walnut(s)'; h. *pisutatio* 'pistachio'

REVIEW 2:

a. *tyañsu* 'chance'; b. *aid(e)ia* 'idea'; c. *sisutemu* 'system'; d. *akusesu* 'access'; e. *suteetasu* 'status'; f. *apurooti* 'approach'; g. *ideorogii* 'ideology'; h. *saidosuteppu* 'sidestep'; i. nettowaaku 'network'; j. *raihusutairu* 'lifestyle'; k. *aideñt(e)it(e)i* 'identity'; l. *huroñt(e)ia* 'frontier'; m. *iñisiat(e)ivu* 'initiative'; n. *dainamikkusu* 'dynamics'

LESSON 5

Lessons 5 through 8 will introduce the forty-six *hiragana* symbols that are regularly used in modern Japanese writing. We will also introduce two additional *hiragana* symbols that are no longer in common use, as well as some historical and special spellings.

Many verbals and adjectivals are written with *kanzi* plus *hiragana*, but some are written entirely in *hiragana*. Many nominals are also written with *hiragana*. *Hiragana* is used for all particles, all forms of the copula (e.g. *desu*, *desita*), and inflectional endings of all adjectivals and verbals. In addition, if a verbal that is normally written with a combination of *kanzi* and *hiragana* occurs within (= not initially) in a verbal phrase (e.g. *kudasai* in *mite kudasai*), it is usually written entirely with *hiragana*.

With the introduction of Japanese punctuation marks, you can now read complete Japanese sentences that are written with *katakana* and *hiragana*.

In the following presentation of *hiragana* symbols, each one is accompanied by its *katakana* equivalent as well as romanization spelling.

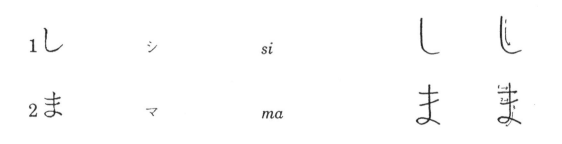

3 す   ス   *su*   す ず

。   *maru* 'end of a sentence'

Maru is normally used at the end of questions as well as statements. The question mark may be used in a question that is written horizontally.

、   *ten* 'comma in a sentence' represents a pause

Examples:

a します。   *Simâsu.* '[I] do/will do it.'

b メモします。   *Mêmo-simasu.* '[I] make/will make a memo.'

c コントロールします。   *Kóñtoròoru-simasu.* '[I] control/will control [it].'

d テニス、しますか。   *Tênisu, simâsu ka.*[1] Do [you] play [lit. do] tennis?'

4 た   タ   *ta*   た だ

Examples:

a しました。   *Simâsita.* '[I] did [it].'

b タイプしました。   *Tâipu-simasita.* '[I] typed [it].'

c ダビングしました。   *Dabíñḡu-simàsita.* '[I] dubbed [it].'

---

1. Word division in the romanization follows procedures established in JSL. Note the lack of any such division in the Japanese writing.

5 か　　カ　　*ka*　　　　か＼　か＼

Examples:

a しますか。　　　　　　　*Simâsu ka.* 'Do/Will [you] do [it]?'

b しましたか。　　　　　　*Simâsita ka.* 'Did [you] do [it]?'
c アナウンスしましたか。　*Anáùñsu-simasita ka.* 'Did [you] announce [it]?'

6 り　　リ　　*ri*　　　　り　　リ＼

7 あ　　ア　　*a*　　　　あ　あ

Examples:

a ありますか。　　　　　　*Arímàsu ka.* 'Are there any?' 'Do [you] have [any]?'

b ありました。　　　　　　*Arímàsita.* 'There was/were [some].'
c ケーキ、ありますか。　　*Kêeki, arímàsu ka.* 'Is [there] any cake?'

8 い　　イ　　*i*　　　　い　い＼

Example:

a いりますか。　　　　　　*Irímàsu ka.* 'Do [you] need [it]?'

9 れ　　レ　　*re*　　　　れ　れ

Example:

a あれ *are* 'that thing (over there)'
'that thing (we both know about)'

10 そ　　ソ *so*

Example:
a それ *sore* 'that thing'

11 と　　ト *to*

Examples:
a ペンとノート *pêñ to nôoto* 'a pen and a notebook'
b あれとそれ *are to sore* 'that thing over there and that thing'

c タイプとコピー *tâipu to kôpii* 'typing and copying'

12 を　　ヲ *o* (as particle only)

Examples:
a それをしますか。 *Soré o simàsu ka.* 'Do/Will [you] do that?'
b テストをしました。 *Tesuto o simâsita.* '[I] took [lit. did] a test.'

13 も　　モ *mo*

Examples:
a それもいります。 *Soré mo irimàsu.* '[I] need that too'
b タイプもします。 *Tâipu mo simasu.* '[I] type too'
c あれもそれもします。 *Aré mo sore mo simàsu.* '[I] do/will do both that (over there) and that.'

d それもあれもあります。

Soré mo are mo arimàsu. '[I] have both that and that (over there).' 'There are both that and that (over there).'

14 は ハ

ha; wa (as particle only)   は ば

Examples:

a ワープロはあります。

Waápuro wa arimàsu. 'A wordprocessor (at least) exists.' 'There is a wordprocessor (at least).'

b コピーはしました。
c テニス、しますか。
d はい、テニスはします。

Kôpii wa simâsita. '[I] copied [it] (at least).'
Tênisu, simâsu ka. 'Do [you] play tennis?'
Hâi, tênisu wa simasu. 'Yes, [I] play tennis (at least).'

15 せ セ

se   せ せ

ぜ ゼ

ze   ぜ ぜ

16 ん ン

n   ん ん

Examples:

a ありません。

Arímasèñ. 'There isn't any.' '[I] don't have [it/any].'

b いりません。
c しません。

Irímasèñ. '[I] don't/won't need [it]'
Simásèñ. '[I] don't/won't do [it]'

SUMMARY

ん	ン		ワ	ラ	リ	ヤ	ま	マ	は	ハ		ナ	た	タ		サ	か	カ	あ	ア
				り	リ			ミ		ヒ		ニ		チ	し	シ		キ	い	イ
					ル	ユ		ム		フ		ヌ		ツ	す	ス		ク		ウ
				れ	レ			メ		ヘ		ネ		テ	せ	セ		ケ		エ
		を	ヲ		ロ	ヨ	も	モ		ホ		ノ	と	ト	そ	ソ		コ		オ

DIACRITICS

The use of *nigori* and *maru* with *hiragana* is parallel to their use with *katakana*. Thus:

HIRAGANA		*KATAKANA*		ROMANIZATION
が	=	ガ	=	*ga* or *ḡa*
じ	=	ジ	=	*zi*
ず	=	ズ	=	*zu*
ぜ	=	ゼ	=	*ze*
ぞ	=	ゾ	=	*zo*
だ	=	ダ	=	*da*
ど	=	ド	=	*do*
ば	=	バ	=	*ba*
ぱ	=	パ	=	*pa*

Examples:

a だれ   *dâre* 'who?'

b どれ   *dôre* 'which one?'

c いかが   *ikâḡa* 'how?'

d だれがしますか。   *Dàre ḡa simasu ka.* 'Who does/will do [it]?'

e これとこれがいります。   *Kore to kore ga irimasu.* '[I] need this and this.'

f まずいコーヒー   *mazûi koohii* 'bad-tasting coffee'

g それはありますが。   *Soré wa arimàsu ḡa.* 'That (at least) is there, but. . . .'

h ぜんぜんありません。   *Zéñzeñ arimasèn.* '[It] is not there at all.' 'There isn't [any] at all.'

READING DRILLS

A　バリエーション・ドリル
1. コピーします。
2. タイプしました。
3. コントロールしました。
4. アナウンスします。
5. ダビングします。
6. メモしました。

B　バリエーション・ドリル
1. ラジオがあります。
2. ワープロもあります。
3. タイプライターはあります。
4. メモをコピーしました。
5. ノートもコピーしました。
6. アナウンサーがインタビューしました。
7. スピーチはダビングします。
8. ボリュームをコントロールします。

C　バリエーション・ドリル
1. それとあれをします。
2. ビールとワインがあります。
3. あれとそれをタイプします。
4. それとそれをアナウンスします。
5. ニュースとスポーツをダビングします。

D　バリエーション・ドリル
1. パイもクッキーもあります。
2. ゴルフもテニスもします。
3. カセットテープもビデオテープもいります。
4. コピーもダビングもしました。
5. ケーキもパイもありました。

E　バリエーション・ドリル
1. ノートもペンもいります。
2. タクシーもバスもあります。
3. ショッピングバッグもハンドバッグもあります。
4. アイスクリームもプリンもあります。
5. コンピューターもタイプライターもいります。

F　バリエーション・ドリル
1. それはしますが、あれはしません。
2. テニスはしますが、ゴルフはしません。
3. ビールはありますがワインはありません。
4. ジャズはダビングしますが、ロックはダビングしません。
5. ノートはコピーしますが、パンフレットはコピーしません。

WRITING PRACTICE

(1) Practice writing statements contrasting two individuals, one of whom owns (a) a tent; (b) tapes; (c) a sports car, and the other who doesn't. Use personal names that you can write using katakana.

Example:
Risa-sañ wa, teñto g̃a arimasu g̃a, Terii-sañ wa arimaseñ.

(2) Practice writing statements identifying an individual who needs (a) a note[book]; (b) a pen; (c) some cream. Use personal names that you can write using katakana.

Example:
Ereñ-sañ g̃a nooto g̃a irimasu.

HIRAGANA WRITING PRACTICE

	1	2	3		
si	し				
ma	一	二	ま		
su	一	す			
[maru]	o				
[ten]	`				
ka	つ	カ	か		
ri	l	り			
a	一	十	あ		
i	l	い			

	1	2			
re	l	れ			
so	そ				
to	ヽ	と			
(w)o	一	￡	を		
mo	し	も	も		
ha	l	に	は		
se	一	ナ	せ		
n	ん				

LESSON 6

17 こ　　コ　　　　*ko*　　　　　　　こ　　　こ

ご　　ゴ　　　　*go*

Examples:

a これ　　　　　*kore* 'this thing'
b ここ　　　　　*koko* 'this place'
c そこ　　　　　*soko* 'that place'
d あそこ　　　　*asoko*
e あすこ　　　　or *asuko* 'that place (over there)'

18 さ　　サ　　　　*sa*　　　　　　さ　　　さ

ざ　　ザ　　　　*za*

Examples:

a ミラーさん　　　*Mîraa-sañ* 'Mr/s. Miller'
b ございません。　*Gozáimasèñ.* 'There isn't [any].⁺'

19 て　　テ　　　　*te*　　　　　て　　　で

で　　デ　　　　*de*

Examples:

a ボールペンです。　*Boórupeñ dèsu.* '[It] is a ball-point pen.'

b ホテルまでです。   *Hôteru made desu.* '[It] is up to the hotel.' '[It] is/goes as far as the hotel.'

c どれですか。   *Dôre desu ka.* 'Which [one] is it?'

20 け   ケ   *ke*   け げ

げ   げ   *ge*

Examples:

a それだけ   *sore dake* 'that much' '[to] that extent'

b スミスですけど。   *Sûmisu desu kedo.* 'It's Smith, but....' '[I] am Smith, but....'

21 の   ノ   *no*   の の

Examples:

a スミスさんのボールペン   *Sûmisu-sañ no 'boorupen'* 'Smith's ball-point pen'

b カーターさんのです。   *Kâataa-sañ no desu.* '[It] is Carter's.'

c いいのがあります。   *Îi no ga arimasu.* 'There's a good one.'

d ドイツのスポーツカーです。   *Dôitu no supóotu·kàa desu.* '[It] is a German sports car.'

22 な   ナ   *na*   な な

Examples:

a こんなペン   *kóñna pèñ* 'pens like this'

b なかなかいいです。   *Nakánaka ìi desu.* '[It] is quite good.'

c あなた   *anâta* 'you'

23 よ　　　ヨ　　　*yo*　　　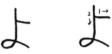

Examples:

a しますよ。

b ありませんでしたよ。

Simâsu yo. ʼ[I] do/will do [it] (I tell you).ʼ

Arímasèñdesita yo. [It] wasn't there (I tell you).ʼ ʼ[I] didn't have [it], (I tell you).ʼ

24 ね　　　ネ　　　*ne*

Examples:

a いいですね。

b スペインですね。

Îi desu ne. ʼ[It] is OK, right?ʼ

Supêiñ desu ne. ʼ[It] is Spain, right?ʼ

25 え　　　エ　　　*e*

Examples:

a いえ

ie ʼnoʼ

26 く　　　ク　　　*ku*

ぐ　　　グ　　　*gu*

Examples:

a すぐしますよ。

b すぐそばです。

c よくないです。

Sûḡu simâsu yo. ʼ[I] will do [it] right away.ʼ

Sûḡu sôba desu. ʼ[It] is right near by.ʼ

Yôku nâi desu. ʼ[It] is not good.ʼ

27 つ   ッ   *tu*   つ つ

づ   ヅ   *zu*

Examples:

a いつ   *îtu* 'when?'

b いくつ   *îkutu* 'how many'

28 お   オ   *o*   お お

Examples:

a おつり   *oturi* 'change'

b おととい   *otótòi* 'day before yesterday'

29 き   キ   *ki*   き き

ぎ   ギ   *gi*

Examples:

a できます。   *Dekímàsu.* '[I] can do [it]' '[I] will be finished.'

30 う   ウ   *u*   う う

SUMMARY

ん ン	ワ	ラ	ヤ	ま マ	は ハ	な ナ	た タ	さ サ	か カ	あ ア
		り リ		ミ	ヒ	ニ	チ	し シ	き キ	い イ
		ル	ユ	ム	フ	ヌ	つ ツ	す ス	く ク	う ウ
		れ レ		メ	ヘ	ね ネ	て テ	せ セ	け ケ	え エ
	を ヲ	ロ	よ ヨ	も モ	ホ	の ノ	と ト	そ ソ	こ コ	お オ

LONG CONSONANTS

The *hiragana* representation of long consonants is parallel to that of *katakana*: a reduced っ , the *hiragana* equivalent of ッ , precedes a symbol representing a syllable that begins with the consonant that is being lengthened. Thus:

$$\underline{\quad}っけ \;=\; \underline{\quad}ッケ \;=\; \underline{\quad}kke$$
$$\underline{\quad}っし \;=\; \underline{\quad}ッシ \;=\; \underline{\quad}ssi$$
$$\underline{\quad}っつ \;=\; \underline{\quad}ッツ \;=\; \underline{\quad}ttu$$
$$\underline{\quad}っぱ \;=\; \underline{\quad}ッパ \;=\; \underline{\quad}ppa$$

In *hiragana*, the only long consonants that are normally written this way are *tt*, *kk*, *ss*, and *pp*. Other such combinations that occur are present only in loanwords and therefore would not ordinarily be written in *hiragana*.[1]

Examples:

[1]. See Lesson 4.

おいしかったです。	*Oísikatta desu.* '[It] was tasty.'
よかったですね。	*Yôkatta desu ne!* '[It] was good, wasn't it?'
あさってしますよ。	*Asâtte simàsu yo.* '[I] will do [it] the day after tomorrow (I tell you).'
もっといります。	*Môtto irímàsu.* '[I] will need more.' '[I] need more.'

LONG VOWELS

Unlike the *katakana* representation of long vowels, which uses a straight line to indicate length, the *hiragana* representation regularly specifies a long vowel by writing a second *hiragana* symbol. Thus:

Hiragana	*Katakana*	Romanization
いい	イー	*ii*
まあ	マー	*maa*
きい	キー	*kii*
くう	クー	*kuu*

However, what is pronounced as *ee* (and so written in JSL romanization) is usually written as *ei* in *hiragana*. Romanization in this text will hereafter reflect the spelling and tradition rather than pronunciation.

Examples:
きれい	*kîrei* (JSL *kiree*) 'pretty'
たいてい	*taitei* (JSL *taitee*) 'usually'

Following are examples of the rare cases where the *hiragana* spelling coincides with a long *e* in the pronunciation. The usual spelling of long *e*:

ええ	*èe* 'yes'
ねえ	*nêe* 'isn't it the case?'

Long *o* (romanized *oo*) is spelled with a final う in *hiragana*. In this case, the *oo* romanization will be continued in this text, conforming to both pronunciation and tradition.

Examples:

どう	*dôo* 'how?'
どうぞ	*dôozo* 'please'
どうも	*dôomo* 'in every way'
どういたしまして	*dôo itasimasite* 'don't mention it'
きのう	*kinoo* 'yesterday'
そうです	*sôo desu* 'is as suggested'
こちらのほう	*kotíra no hòo* 'is this way'
ありがとう	*arîḡatoo* 'thank you'
おはようございます	*oháyoo gozaimàsu* 'good morning'

Long *o* in only a few words is spelled in *hiragana* with final お (for example, おおきい *oókii* 'is big'; とおい *tooi* 'is far'), and only such words unambiguously correspond to *oo* in romanization. In all other instances, the occurrence of a *hiragana* symbol representingan *o*-final syllable followed by う, may corrrespond to *oo* or *ou*.

For example, *hiragana* そう = *sôo* 'that way' or *sou* 'suit', 'meet'. Ambiguity is resolved by context in the written language and by pronunciation (as well as context) in the spoken language.

READING DRILLS

A   リスポンス・ドリル
1. いつしましたか。
   きのうしました。
2. だれがしますか。
   ディレクターがしました。
3. いつできますか。
   あさってできます。
4. だれがアナウンスしますか。
   スポークスマンがアナウンスします。
5. おとといしましたか。
   きのうしました。

B   リスポンス・ドリル
1. ペンありますか。
   はい、ありますよ。
2. スミスさん、いますか。
   はい、いますよ。
3. ミラーさん、いませんか。
   はい、いませんよ。
4. タイプライター、ありませんね。
   はい、ありませんよ、
5. ワープロもありましたね。
   いえ、ありませんでしたよ。
6. スーツケースがありますね。
   はい、ありますよ。

C   リスポンス・ドリル
1. ベイリーさんはメキシコです。
   メキシコのどこですか。
2. ホワイトさんはアメリカです。

アメリカのどこですか。
3. カーターさんはイギリスです。
イギリスのどこですか。
4. ルグランさんはフランスです。
フランスのどこですか。
5. ミラーさんはイタリアです。
イタリアのどこですか。
6. ブラウンさんはスペインです。
スペインのどこですか。

D　リスポンス・ドリル
1. あれはガスのメーターですか。
はい、あのメーターはガスのです。
2. あれは、テレビのスタジオですか。
はい、あのスタジオはテレビのです。
3. それはワンウェーのサインですか。
はい、そのサインはワンウェーのです。
4. これはトヨタのマークですか。
はい、このマークはトヨタのです。
5. あれはフランスのスターのポートレートですか。
はい、あのポートレートはフランスのスターのです。
6. これはウォークマンのバッテリーですか。
はい、このバッテリーはウォークマンのです。

E　バリエーション・ドリル
1. こんなペンもそんなノートもありません。
2. もっといいのももっときれいなのもありません。
3. テニスもゴルフもしません。
4. おいしいアイスクリームもパイもありません。
5. ミラーさんのもウォーカーさんのもここです。
6. ここのもあそこのもよくありませんでした。
7. グレーのもグリーンのもそれだけです。

8. あそこのビールもワインもおいしくなかったです。

WRITING PRACTICE

(1) Practice writing questions regarding location of individuals. Use personal names and place names you can write using *katakana* introduced in Lessons 1 and 2.

Example: スーザンさんは、ミズーリです。

(2) Practice writing statements about the ownership of certain items. Use personal names and object names you can write using *katakana* introduced in Lessons 1 and 2.

Example: ハリーのロールスロイスです。

HIRAGANA WRITING PRACTICE

	1	2	3	4	
ko	＼	こ			
sa	一	さ	さ		
te	て				
ke	し	い	け		
no	の				
na	一	ナ	な	な	
yo	一	よ			
ne	し	ね			
e	、	え			

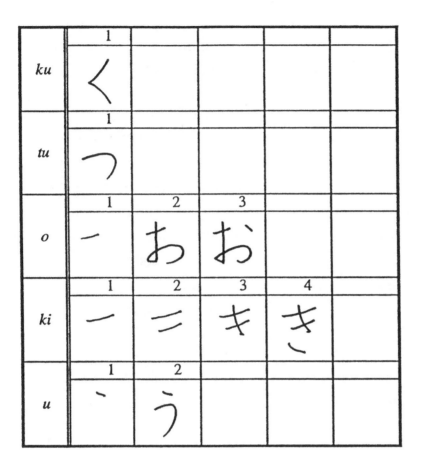

LESSON 7

HURIGANA

Japanese is written with a specific prescribed combination of *kana* and Chinese characters (or *kanji*, which will be introduced systematically starting Lesson 9). When *kanji* reading is expected to be unknown or ambiguous to the reader, a small *hiragana* is written beside the *kanji* to aid the reader. The *hiragana* with this special function is called *hurigana*.

There are three possible reasons for assuming the readers' difficulty in reading a given *kanji* sequence: it includes a *kanji* that is so rare that most native speakers do not know; a portion or the whole combination has a very unusual reading in a given context; the reader is assumed to have the *kanji* knowledge which is less than that of an educated adult native speaker (as in the case of a child or a non-Japanese who is at her/his initial stage of studying the writing system.

Hurigana will be provided hereafter for the sequences which have already been introduced in JSL, and which are ordinarily written in *kanji*.

Examples:

a 三(さん)　　　　　　　　　　*sañ* 'three'

b 前(まえ)　　　　　　　　　　*mâe* 'front'

c 先(さき)　　　　　　　　　　*saki* 'ahead'

d 駅(えき)　　　　　　　　　　*êki* 'station'

e 本   *hôn* 'book'

f 建物   *tatêmono* 'building'

g 上野   *Ueno* (section of Tokyo)

h 大阪   *Oosaka* 'Osaka'

31 へ   ヘ   *he; e* (as particle only)   ヘ ヘ

　 べ   ベ   *be*

　 ぺ   ペ   *pe*

Examples:
a このへん   *kono hen* 'around here'
b ホテルへ   *hôteru e* 'to the hotel'

32 ら   ラ   *ra*   ら ら

Example:
a いくら   *îkura* 'how much'

33 ち   チ   *ti*   ち ち

　 ぢ   ヂ   *zi*[1]

Examples:
a どちら   *dôtira* 'where?'

1. The hiragana ぢ is used only in a small number of words. The use of this hiragana will be explained in Lesson 8.

b どちらへ   *dôtira e* 'to where?'
c うち   *uti* 'home'
d こっち   *kotti* 'this way'

34 に   ニ   ni

Examples:

a そこにあります。   *Sokó ni arimàsu.* '[It] is there.'
b ここにもあります。   *Kokó ni mo arimàsu.* '[It] is here, too.'

35 ほ   ホ   ho

ぼ   ボ   bo

ぽ   ポ   po

Examples:

a こちらのほう   *kotíra no hòo* 'toward this way'
b ほとんど   *hotôñdo* 'almost'
c 一本 (いっぽん)   *îp-poñ* 'one long cylindrical object'

36 や   ヤ   ya

Examples:

a やっぱり   *yappàri* 'after all'
b いや、あちらのほうです。   *Iya, atíra no hòo desu.* 'No, [it]'s toward that way over there.'

37 ふ   フ   hu

ぶ	ブ	*bu*
ぷ	プ	*pu*

Example:

a ふりがな *huríg̀ana* 'reading marks on kanji' [NB in parens??]

38 ゆ　　ユ　　*yu*　　ゆ　ゆ

Example:

a 雪（ゆき） *yukî* 'snow'

39 る　　ル　　*ru*　　る　ろ

Example:

a 歩（ある）きます。 *Arúkimàsu.* '[I] will walk.' '[I] walk.'

SUMMARY

ん ン		ワ	ら ラ	や ヤ	ま マ	は ハ	な ナ	た タ	さ サ	か カ	あ ア
			り リ		ミ	ヒ	に ニ	ち チ	し シ	き キ	い イ
			る ル	ゆ ユ	ム	ふ フ	ヌ	つ ツ	す ス	く ク	う ウ
			れ レ		メ	へ ヘ	ね ネ	て テ	せ セ	け ケ	え エ
	を ヲ	ロ	よ ヨ	も モ	ほ ホ	の ノ	と ト	そ ソ	こ コ	お オ	

CONSONANT + *y* + VOWEL

The combination of a *hiragana* symbol that represents a syllable consisting of consonant + *i* followed immediately by a reduced symbol (i.e., smaller and lower, or smaller and to the right) that represents *ya*, *yu*, or *yo*, indicates a single syllable romanized as consonant + *y* + vowel. This parallels the *katakana* representations exactly.[2]

Thus, きや is equivalent to the two-syllable sequence romanized as *kiya*, but きゃ is equivalent to the single syllable romanized as *kya*.

Including only *hiragana* symbols which have already been introduced, the following combinations occur:

きゃ *kya* ぎゃ *gya* しゃ *sya* じゃ *zya* ちゃ *tya* にゃ *nya* りゃ *rya*
きゅ *kyu* ぎゅ *gyu* しゅ *syu* じゅ *zyu* ちゅ *tyu* にゅ *nyu* りゅ *ryu*
きょ *kyo* ぎょ *gyo* しょ *syo* じょ *zyo* ちょ *tyo* にょ *nyo* りょ *ryo*

2. See Lesson 3.

Examples:

a きょう   *kyôo* 'today'

b きのうでしょう。   *Kinôo desyoo.* '[It] is probably yesterday.'

c そうじゃないでしょう。   *Sôo zya nâi desyoo.* '[It] is probably not that way.'

d いらっしゃいます。   *Irássyaimàsu.* '[S/he] is there. ↑'

e これでしょう。   *Koré desyòo.* '[It] is probably this.'

f しましょうか。   *Simásyòo ka.* 'Shall I do [it]?'

g ちょうどいいでしょう。   *Tyoódo ìi desyoo.* '[It] is probably just right.'

h ちょっとすみません。   *Tyôtto sumímasèñ.* 'Excuse [me] for a bit.'

i いらっしゃいませ。   *Irássyaimàse.* 'Welcome (to the shop).'

j まっすぐでしょう。   *Massûg̈u desyoo.* '[It] is probably straight.'

k つきあたりでしょうか。   *Tukíatari desyòo ka.* 'Do [you] suppose [it]'s a deadend?'

l だいじょうぶです。   *Daízyòobu desu.* '[It] is all right.'

READING DRILLS

A　ヴァリーション・ドリル

1. どこがいいでしょうか。
2. ここのパイはまずいでしょうか。
3. あそこは、プリンもおいしいでしょうか。
4. あそこはデパートでしょうか。
5. トイレはどこでしょうか。
6. あのデパートは、サービスがいいでしょうか。

B　リスポンス・ドリル

1. スミスさんはインドじゃないでしょうか。
　　　　あ、インドですよ。
2. ミラーさんはアメリカじゃありませんか。
　　　　いえ、カナダでしょう。
3. ジョンソンさんはスペインですね。
　　　　いや、イタリアじゃありませんか。
4. ピーターソンさんはフランスですか。
　　　　いえ、ソビエトでしょう。
5. ミネズさんはオーストラリアでしょうねえ。
　　　　そうでしょうねえ。

C　ヴァリエーション・ドリル

1. あさって行きたいんですが...
2. すぐしたくないんですが...
3. きょう、いらっしゃいませんが...
4. ここでまがりたいんですが...
5. あそこに行きたいんですが...
6. ちょっとだけいただきたいんですが...
7. あしたも来たいんですが...

D　コンビネーション・ドリル

1. タイプしました。コピーしました。

　　　タイプして、コピーしました。

2. 行きました。ダビングしました。

　　　行って、ダビングしました。

3. まっすぐ行きました。ユーターンしました。

　　　まっすぐ行って、ユーターンしました。

4. コンピューターを使いました。教えました。

　　　コンピューターを使って、教えました。

5. もっと先まで行きました。使いました。

　　　もっと先まで行って、使いました。

6. アイスクリームをいただきました。食べました。

　　　アイスクリームをいただいて、食べました。

7. レストランで食べました。来ました。

　　　レストランで食べて来ました。

8. 歩きました。来ました。

　　　歩いて来ました。

E　リスポンス・ドリル

1. 行ってまいります。

　　　行ってらっしゃい。

　　　行っていらっしゃい。

2. ただいま。

　　　お帰りなさい。

3. こんにちは。

こんにちは。
4. おはようございます。
おはようございます。
5. さようなら。
おつかれさま。
6. どこでしょうか。
どこでしょうかねえ。
7. はい、どうぞ。
いただきます。 ... ごちそうさま。

F　リスポンス・ドリル

1. どこまで行きましたか。

パークビールまで行きました。

2. どこで曲がりましたか。

つきあたりで曲がりました。

3. どこでしましたか。
イギリスでしました。

4. どのへんにいますか。

入口のへんにいます。

5. どこまでできましたか。
16ページまでできました。

G　コンビネーション・ドリル

1. そこへ行きました。

あそこへ行きました。

そこへもあそこへも行きました。

2. フランスにあります。
ドイツにあります。

ドイツにもフランスにもあります。

3. ここでします。

　　そこでします。

　　　ここでもそこでもします。

4. そのレストランで食^たべました。

　　あのレストランで食^たべました。

　　　そのレストランでもあのレストランでも食^たべました。

WRITING PRACTICE

(1) Fill in the blanks with appropriate place names. Consult a world atlas, if necessary.

ビッグ・ベンは＿＿＿＿＿＿＿にあります。

ゴールデン・ゲート・ブリッジは＿＿＿＿＿＿にあります。

コペンハーゲンは＿＿＿＿＿にあります。

オアフは＿＿＿＿にあります。

フィレンツェは＿＿＿＿＿にあります。

ヴァンクーヴァーは＿＿＿＿＿にあります。

ユージンは＿＿＿＿＿＿にあります。

スロバキアもギリシャも＿＿＿＿＿にあります。

スーダンもザンビアも＿＿＿＿＿にあります。

HIRAGANA WRITING PRACTICE

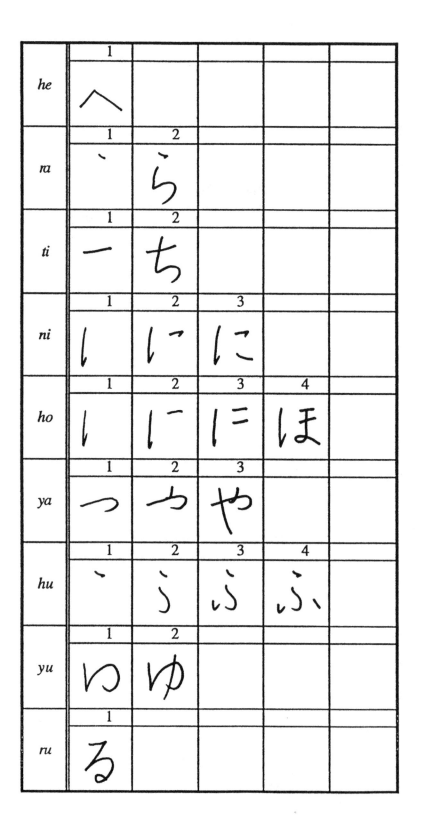

	1	2	3	4	
he	へ				
ra	`	ら			
ti	一	ち			
ni	し	に	に		
ho	し	に	に	ほ	
ya	つ	や	や		
hu	`	ふ	ふ	ふ	
yu	ゆ	ゆ			
ru	る				

LESSON 8

40 み   ミ   mi

Examples:

a すみません。   *Sumímasèñ.* '[I] am sorry.' 'Excuse [me].'

b みんな   *miñna* 'everybody

c おやすみなさい。   *Oyasumi nasai.* 'Good night.'

41 わ   ワ   wa

Examples:

a 悪い^{わる}です。   *Warûi desu.* '[It] is bad.'

b おまわりさん   *omâwarisan* 'policeman'

42 ろ   ロ   ro

Examples:

a いるごろ   *itu goro* 'about when?'

b ふろしき   *hurosiki* 'wrapping cloth'

43 め   メ   me

Examples:

a やめました。   *Yamémàsita.* '[I] quit.'

b だめです。   *Damê desu.* '[It] is no good.'

44 む   ム   *mu*   む む

Example:

a 向こうまで   *mukóo màde* 'up to over there'

45 ひ   ヒ   *hi*   ひ ひ

Example:

a 一つ   *hitô-tu* 'one unit'

46 ぬ   ヌ   *nu*   ぬ ぬ

Example:

a いぬ1   *inu* 'dog'

HISTORICAL SPELLING

1. Modern *kana* spelling (*síñkanazùkai*) is closely correlated with modern Japanese pronunciation. Except for the particles *wa*,2 *e* and *o* (represented as は, へ, and を), and the ええ/えい, and おお/おう alternations, the *kana* spelling of Japanese is almost completely predictable on the basis of present-day standard pronunciation.

However, this close correlation that exists today is the result of writing reforms that were adopted in 1947. Prior to those reforms, *kana* spelling

1. This word is more commonly represented by kanzi.
2. That is, phrase particle *wa* (は), not the sentence particle.

often represented an earlier period of the spoken language (cf. English spellings like 'knight,' 'through,' etc., which represent earlier pronunciations). For example, the *kana* sequence けふ (*ke-hu*) was a former *kana* spelling for the sequence now written きょう (*kyôo*). This means that in order to read material written before *sinkanazukai* was adopted, students must familiarize themselves with the different *kana* spelling conventions of the period.

In the changeover from historical to modern *kana* spelling, some symbols were lost completely:

a)   *Hiraḡana* ゐ

    =   *Katakana* ヰ

These symbols are traditionally listed in the second box of the *w*-row (i.e., under わ/ ワ in the table of fifty sounds) as equivalents of い/ イ that occur only in the historical spelling of certain words.

Example:
Modern: います (イマス); Historical spelling: ゐます (ヰマス) 'be'

B)   *Hiraḡana* ゑ

    =   *Katakana* ヱ

These symbols are traditionally listed in the fouth box of the *w*-row, as equivalents of え / エ. Again, these symbols occur only in the historical spellings of certain words.

Example:
Modern: え (エ); Historical spelling:ゑ (ヱ) 'picture'

2. The occurrence of ち / チ and つ / ツ with *nigori* is also a feature of historical spelling. Some words currently written with じ and ず formerly had ぢ and づ in their kana spelling, but the historical spelling differenciation was given up. Thus:

Historical Spelling		Modern Spelling	
ぢ (ヂ)	↘		
じ (ジ)	→	じ (ジ)	
づ (ヅ)	↘		
ず (ズ)	→	ず (ズ)	

However, even in modern spelling, these historical combinations may survive in compounds when the *zi* and *zu* syllables are obviously derived from *ti* and *tu*.

Examples:

ち
血   *ti*   'blood'

はなぢ
鼻血   *hanazi*   'nose bleed'

つつ
包み   *tutúmi*   'bundle'
こづつ   *kozûtumi*   'small package'
小包(み)

SPECIAL SYMBOLS

1.As a substitute for writing a given *hiragana* symbol twice in succession within the same word, the symbol ヽ , functioning as '*kana* ditto marks,' may replace the repeated symbol.3 Thus:

ああ or あヽ		*âa*	'oh'
ここ or こヽ		*koko*	'this place'

This symbol may occur with *nigori*, indicating that the previous syllable is to be repeated in its *nigori* form. The previous syllable may or may not have *nigori*. Thus:

いかが or いかゞ	*ikâḡa*	'how?'
ごご or ごゞ	*gôḡo*	'P.M.'

2. In vertical writing, the repetition of a sequence of more than one *kana* within the same word is indicated by an elongated symbol that resembles the *hiragana* equivalent of *ku*.4 This symbol may also occur with *nigori*. Thus:

も	or	も	*môsimosi*	'hello (on the telephone)'
し		し		'say there!'
も		〈		
し				

と	or	と	*tokidoki*	'sometimes'
き		き		
ど		〈		
き				

3.This does not apply to *katakana*.

4. This does not apply to katakana.

3. In horizontal writing, such repetition of a sequence is indicated by an elongated symbol that resembles the *hiragana* equivalent of *he*. Thus:

もしもし

or

もし〳〵   *mosimosi*   'hello (on the telephone) 'say there!'

ときどき

or

とき〳〵   *tokidoki*   'sometimes'

SUMMARY

KATAKANA

ン n	ワ wa	ラ ra	ヤ ya	マ ma	ハ ha	ナ na	タ ta	サ sa	カ ka	ア a
		リ ri		ミ mi	ヒ hi	ニ ni	チ ti	シ si	キ ki	イ i
		ル ru	ユ yu	ム mu	フ hu	ヌ nu	ツ tu	ス su	ク ku	ウ u
		レ re		メ me	ヘ he	ネ ne	テ te	セ se	ケ ke	エ e
	ヲ o	ロ ro	ヨ yo	モ mo	ホ ho	ノ no	ト to	ソ so	コ ko	オ o

HIRAGANA

ん ン	わ ワ	ら ラ	や ヤ	ま マ	は ハ	な ナ	た タ	さ サ	か カ	あ ア
		り リ		み ミ	ひ ヒ	に ニ	ち チ	し シ	き キ	い イ
		る ル	ゆ ユ	む ム	ふ フ	ぬ ヌ	つ ツ	す ス	く ク	う ウ
		れ レ		め メ	へ ヘ	ね ネ	て テ	せ セ	け ケ	え エ
	を ヲ	ろ ロ	よ ヨ	も モ	ほ ホ	の ノ	と ト	そ ソ	こ コ	お オ

VOCABULARY PRACTICE

Remember that you should rely on *hiragana* for reading the following *kanji* items.

さっぽろ 札幌	よこはま 横浜	おおさか 大阪	とうきょう 東京	めじろ 目白
しんじゅく 新宿	とらもん 虎の門	なごや 名古屋	こうべ 神戸	ふくおか 福岡

READING DRILLS

A　リスポンス・ドリル

1.　ブラウンさんはパリですね。
　　　　いや、ロンドンじゃなかったですか。

2.　ホワイトさんはシカゴですね。
　　　　いや、サン・フランシスコじゃなかったですか。

3.　カーターさんはベルリンですね。
　　　　いや、モスクワじゃなかったですか。

4.　木村さんはソウルですね。

　　　　いや、北京じゃなかったですか。

5.　中村さんは大阪ですね。

　　　　いや、東京じゃなかったですか。

6.　宮路さんはヨーロッパですね。
　　　　いや、オーストラリアじゃなかったですか。

B　リスポンス・ドリル

1.　三日ぐらいいますか。

　　　　　　いえ、二日だけです。

2.　十日ぐらいいますか。

　　　　　　いえ、九日だけです。

3.　八日ぐらいいますか。

　　　　　　いえ、七日だけです。

4.　六日ぐらいいますか。

　　　　　　いえ、五日だけです。

5.　十五日ぐらいいますか。

　　　　　　いえ、十四日だけです。

6.　二日ぐらいいますか。

　　　　　　いえ、一日だけです。

C　コンビネーション・ドリル

1.　山本さんは札幌です。カーターさんは名古屋です。
　　　山本さんは札幌で、カーターさんは名古屋です。

2.　西坂さんは神戸です。ミラーさんは東京です。
　　　西坂さんは神戸で、ミラーさんは東京です。

3.　ブラウンさんは新宿です。坂本さんは目白です。
　　　ブラウンさんは新宿で、坂本さんは目白です。

4　犬山さんは横浜です。スミスさんは虎の門です。
　　　犬山さんは横浜で、スミスさんは虎の門です。

5.　道子さんは大阪です。デイブさんは福岡です。
　　　道子さんは大阪で、デイブさんは福岡です。

6.　たかしさんは香港です。スーザンさんは北京です。
　　　たかしさんは香港で、スーザンさんは北京です。

D　バリエーション・ドリル

1.　これから名古屋まで行ってきます。

2.　これから大阪まで行ってきます。

3.　これから横浜まで行ってきます。

4.　これから日比谷まで行ってきます。

5.　これから虎の門まで行ってきます。

6.　これから目白まで行ってきます。

7.　これから学校まで行ってきます。

8.　これから図書館まで行ってきます。

E　バリエーション・ドリル

1.　だめですねえ、わたし。

2.　おもしろいですねえ、この本。

3.　おまわりさんですねえ、あれ。

4.　おとなりでしたねえ、パークビル。

5. つきあたりですよ、この道。

6. トイレですねえ、むこう。

7 どちらですか、先生。

8. 出口ですか、後ろ。

F　バリエーション・ドリル

1. ここから目白までタクシーでどのぐらいかかりますか。

2. みんなヨーロッパへ行きますか。

3. ずいぶんたくさんテープを買いましたね。

4. みんなここにいましたか。

5. ワープロをだれが使いましたか。

6. バスであそこまで行きましたか。

G　バリエーション・ドリル

1. おもしろかったけれど、ぜんぜんできませんでした。

2. おいしかったでけれど、ぜんぜん高くありませんでした。

3. 小さかったけれど、ぜんぜん安くありませんでした。

4. 安かったけれど、ぜんぜんまずくなかったです。

5. やさしかったけれど、ぜんぜんおもしろくなかったです。

H　リスポンス・ドリル

1. 十時にはいらっしゃいますね。

　　　いえ、あしたは八時ですが。

2.　八時にはいらっしゃいますね。

　　　　いえ、あさっては九時ですが。

3.　一時にはいらっしゃいますね。

　　　　いえ、きょうは三時ですが。

4.　七時にはいらっしゃいますね。

　　　　いえ、あしたは十一時ですが。

5.　三時にはいらっしゃいますね。

　　　　いえ、きょうは三時半ですが。

6.　四時にはいらっしゃいますね。

　　　　いえ、あさっては六時ごろですが。

I　バリエーション・ドリル

1.　宮路さんはヨーロッパへ行きましたが、わたしはやっぱりやめました。

2.　ミラーさんはタイプしましたが、木村さんはやっぱりしませんでした。

3.　西坂さんはプリンでしたが、ホワイトさんはやっぱりアイスクリームでした。

4.　あのスポースカーはグレーでしたが、坂本さんのはグリーンでした。

5.　ボンは雨でしたが、パリはやっぱり雪でした。

6.　パークビルはすぐそばでしたが、ホテルはやっぱりもっとむこうでした。

WRITING PRACTICE

(1)Identify a local establishment whose names you would write in *katakana*where the following items are good: a. hamburger; b. pizza; c. ice cream; d. frozen yoghurt; e. fried chicken; f. coffee; g. steak; h. home-made dessert.

Example:

ハンバーガーは、バーガーキングがおいしいです。

a.

b.

c.

d.

e.

f.

g.

h.

(2) Respond to the following questions in Japanese. Remember that you need not repeat everything in the question to make your answer complete. You should be able to answer these questions without writing any *kanzi*.

1.　　あなたの名前を教えてください。5

5.If you ordinarily write your name in Chinese characters, do so here. Put the *hurigana* using *hiragana*.

2a.　あなたの学校<ruby>学校<rt>がっこう</rt></ruby>はどこにありますか。

b.　<ruby>学生<rt>がくせい</rt></ruby>はたくさんいますか。

3a.　どんなスポーツをよくしますか。

b.　どこでしますか。

c.　だれとしますか。

4a.　コンピュータがありますか。

b.　どんなタイプのですか。

HIRAGANA WRITING PRACTICE

	1	2			
mi	み	み			
wa	l	わ			
ro	ろ				
me	l	め			
mu	ー	む	む		
hi	ひ				
nu	l	ぬ			

LESSON 9A

This lesson begins the introduction to *kanzi*. Each lesson will be divided into section A and Section B, and together will introduce 25 kanzi. Section A contains 13 new kanzi, Section B contains 12.

A single *kanzi* may represent two or more different sequences of sounds. The readings for kanzi are divided into the *on*-readings, which resemble the Chinese sounds the *kanzi* represented when it was borrowed into Japanese; and the *kun*-reading, which represents the Japanese sounds of words the *kanzi* represents. The *on*-readings are given in capital letters, and the *kun*-readings are given in lower case letters.[1] Personal names, however, will be written with a capital letter at the initial position followed by small letters regardless of the *on/kun* distinction. *Kanzi* which are reintroduced with new readings are marked with an asterisk. Each of those additional readings will also be marked with an asterisk (*).

Each *kanzi* is numbered in the order of its introduction in this text. It also is accompanied by another reference number when it is introduced for the first time. The N___ number is the reference number from Nelson's *Japanese English Character Dictionary*. You will learn later on how to use dictionaries in order to look up new *kanzi* you encounter.

Words and expressions which contain the newly introduced kanzi and are already introduced in JSL are listed following the *kanzi* and its reading(s). Some expressions which are not introduced in JSL, but are useful are also introduced in this portion. They are marked with a plus sign (+) if they are to be learned, with a white star (☆), if they are for reference only. The English equivalents, if given, are listed to the right of the readings, but they are not marked by single quotation.

---

[1]. These readings will not be italicized.

1 一　　　　hito　　　　　　　　　　　　one

　　N1　　hito-(tu)

　　　　ITI/'IP-'IT-'IS-'IK-/

　　　　一つ　　　　hito-tu　　　　one (unit); one year of age

　　　　一ページ　　ITI-peezi　　　one page; page one

　　　　一ドル　　　ITI-doru　　　　one dollar

　　　　一セント　　IS-sento　　　　one cent

1. 一つ
2. 一つある。
3. 一つだけです。
4. 一ページにあります。
5. 一ドルです。
6. もう一ドルありませんか。
7. 一セントだけです。

2 二　　　　　　　　　huta-(tu)　　　　　two

　　N273　　　　　　NI

　　　　二つ　　　　huta-tu　　　　two (units); two years of age

　　　　二インチ　　NI-INTI　　　　two inches

　　　　二センチ(メートル)

　　　　　　　　　NI-senti(meetoru)　two centimeters

　　　　二キロメートル

　　　　　　　　　NI-kiromeetoru　two kilometers

1. 二つ
2. 二つございます。
3. 二つでございますね。
4. スーツケースが二つある。
5. そんなのは二つだけじゃないですか。
6. 一つ二ドルじゃなかったでしょうか。
7. 一インチは二センチぐらいでしょう?

3 十 to/'too/   ten
    N768 too   ten (units); ten years of age
         ZYUU
         二十   NIZYUU   twenty

1. 十
2. 十いります。
3. あと十ですね。
4. クリップが十あります。
5. 十一
6. 二十セント
7. 二十一ドルでした。
8. やっぱり二十ありました。
9. あと二十ページぐらいあります。
10. 一つ二十セントぐらいじゃありませんか。
11. 二十ページありましたが、十ページだけタイプした。

4 日   ka   (classifier for naming and
    N2097   NITI   counting days)
         一日   ITI-NITI   one day
         or tuitati   first day of the month
         二日   hutu-ka   two days; second day of the
                                         month
         十日   too-ka   ten days; tenth day of the month
         二十日   NIZYUU-NITI   twenty days
         or hatu-ka   twentith day of the month

1. 一日
2. 一日だけいます。
3. 一日にタイプしました。
4. ワシントンは一日からです。
5. 二日
6. 二日かかる。

7. 二日にアナウンスしました。

8. 二十日までにしましょう。

9. ジョーンズさんは、二十一日までいらっしゃる。

10. 十一日から二十日までニューヨークにいらっしゃいました。

5　七　nana　　　　　　　　seven

　　N261　nana-(tu)

　　　　　SITI

　　　　　七日　　　　nano-ka　　　seven days; seventh day of the month

1. 七

2. 七つ

3. 七つですか。

4. 七つだけです。

5. そこにケーキが七つあったけど...

6. 七十二

7. 十七

8. ボールが十七いります。

9. 十七マイル

10. 十七日からは、ヨーロッパです。

11. 七日です。

12. 七日までにできますか。

13. 七日までここにいます。

14. 七日はブラウンさんです。

15. 七日ぐらいかかるでしょう。

6　八　ya　　　　　　　　eight

　　N577　yat-(tu)

　　　　　HATI /HAP-'HAT-'HAK-/

　　　　　八日　　　　yoo-ka　　　eight days; eighth day of the month

1. 八つ
2. それを八つですね。
3. 八
4. 八マイル
5. 一つ十八ドルです。
6. 二十八日でしたね。
7. 十八日にもしたいんです。
8. 七じゃありません。八です。
9. 十八センチメートルだけです。
10. 二十八ページからです。
11. それは八十ページにも八十八ページにもありますよ。
12. 八日
13. 八日がゴルフです。
14. 八日までパリにいます。
15. 八日まではここにいません。

7 九 kokono nine
  N146 kokono-(tu)
  KU
          KYUU
    九日 kokono-ka nine days; ninth day of the month

1. 九つ
2. あと九ついります。
3. そのプリンは、九つありますか。
4. カップケーキは十あるけれど、パイは九つだけですねえ。
5. 九
6. 十九ドルのペン
7. 九十じゃありません。十九です。
8. それは九十一ページにありますよ。
9. 十九日

10. 十九日までテストです。

11. 十九日からサマースクールです。

12. サッカーのゲームが十九日にある。

13. 九日

14. 九日と十日

15. 九日からですね。

16. 九日かかりました。

17. 二日から九日までアメリカにいました。

8　三　mi　　　　　　　　　three
　　N8　mit-(tu)
　　　　SAN
　　　　三日　　　mik-ka　　three days; third day of the month

1. 三つ

2. もう三つ

3. そんなのはもう三つありますが。

4. 三日

5. 二日ですか。三日じゃありませんか。

6. 三日から七日まで、サンフランシスコです。

7. 三十

8. 三十三

9. もう三十オーダーしました。

10. 三十ページまでコピーしましょう。

11. 十一はしたけれど、十二と十三はできませんでした。

9　分　wa(karu)　　　　　be comprehensible;　understand
　　N578　HUN/'-PUN/　　　(classifier for naming and counting minutes)
　　　　一分　　IP-PUN　　one minute; minute one of the hour

1. 分かる?
2. 分かります。
3. 分かるでしょう。
4. あまりよく分かりません。
5. 二分
6. 四分
7. 十二分です。
8. あと四分ですね。
9. 二十分ぐらいかかるでしょう。
10. スミスさんは、あそこに二十分いた。
11. ここまでタクシーで三十分かかった。

10 六 mu   six

N283   ROKU/'ROP-'ROK-/
        六分   ROP-PUN   six minutes; minute six of the
                                   hour

1. 六つ
2. 六つできました。
3. こんなコンピューターがもう六ついりますね。
4. 六
5. 十六ドル
6. ちょうど六十分です。
7. そのペンは六ドルです。
8. 六十二はできましたけど、六十三はちょっと...
9. ここからは六分だけだよ。
10. あそこまで、六キロメートルです。

11 五 itu   five

N15   itu-(tu)
       GO

五分	GO-HUN	five minutes; minute five of the hour
十五	ZYUUGO	fifteen; fifteen (units)
	GOZYUU	fifty; fifty (units)

1. 五つ
2. あと五ついりますね。
3. 五
4. 五分
5. 十五ですか。
6. 五センチメートル
7. 一つ五十セントです。
8. あと五十分ですか。
9. 五十五ドルですか。ちょっとありません。すみません。

12 四 yo　　　　　　　　　　four
N1025 yon
yot-(tu)
SI

| 四分 | yon-PUN | four minutes; minute four of the hour |

1. 四つ
2. 四つあります。
3. 四つですね。
4. ハンバーガーが三つとチーズバーガーが四つありました。
5. 四
6. 十三と十四
7. 二十四セントだけ?
8. ドリルの三と四はしましたが、五はできませんでした。

13 **本** HON　　　　　　　　　　book

N96　HON　　　　　　　　　　(classifier for counting long,
　　　/'-BON'-PON/　　　　　　　cylindrical objects)
　　　一本　　　IP-PON　　　　one long, cylindrical object
　　　三本　　　SAN-BON　　　three long, cylindrical objects
　　　日本　　　NIHON
　　　　　　or NIPPON　　　　Japan

1. 本
2. おもしろい本
3. この本はよく分かった。
4. 本もノートもいりますよ。
5. もう五本いります。
6. ペンは三本だけです。
7. 一本二十九セントです。
8. ペンがもう八本いります。
9. これもそれも十本ずつですね。
10. 日本
11. 日本からです。
12. これも日本の本だ。
13. 十四日から二十日まで日本にいました。

READING WRITING EXERCISES

I. Practice writing responses to the questions in A, B and C. Follow the pattern shown in the model in each group.

A.

Model: 二と三ですか。　　　　　　→ 四と五です。

1.　五と六ですか。　→

2.　二十と二十一ですか。　　　　　→

3.　十八と十九ですか。　　　　　　→

4.　七十六と七十七ですか。　　　　→

5.　九十四と九十五ですか。　　　　→

6.　三十七と三十八ですか。　　　　→

B.

Model: あそこまでどのぐらいかかりますか。五分ぐらいですか。
　　　→ あそこまでは五分ぐらいかかるでしょう。

1.　ニューヨークにどのぐらいいますか。八日ぐらいですか。
　　　→

2.　日本にいつからいますか。一日からですか。
　　　→

3.　どこまで分かりましたか。二十ページぐらいまでですか。
　　　→

4.　いつからしますか。九日からですか。
　　　→

5. テニスはいつからしますか。四十分ぐらいからですか。

    →

6. ペンはどのぐらいいりますか。三本ぐらいですか。

    →

7. プリンはいくつありますか。六つぐらいですか。

    →

C.

Model: ジュースが三本ありますが、七本いります。

    → あと四本いります。

1. フィルムが一本ありますが、七本いります。

    →

2. ナイフが五本ありますが、九本いります。

    →

3. ケーキが七つありますが、十いります。

    →

4. クリップが十ありますが、十二いります。

    →

5. ラケットが六本ありますが、七本いります。

    →

6. コンピューターが八つありますが、九ついります。

    →

7. コップが四つありますが、七ついります。

    →

SCANNING EXERCISE

If a current Japanese magazine or newspaper is available to you, look for familiar items and scan for any loan wards written in *katakana*. Write the *katakana* sequences and their English equivalents for at least ten items

ABOUT STROKE ORDER PAGES

At the end of each section of *kañzi*, there will be summary pages in which a handwriting sample for *kañzi* newly introduced in that section is presented. The name of the section is *kakizyun* (書き順) 'stroke order'.

In the first column is the *kañzi* written in block-style hand-writing, called *kaisyo*. This is the style you should use as a model for your writing. Notice that some of the handwriting strokes look quite different from their printed (word-processed) equivalents.

The second column repeats the block-style writing, with the addition of the stroke order in numerals and stroke direction using arrows. Stroke direction is even more important, since a stroke always starts thick but ends in one of several different fixed ways. Study where each stroke begins, and how it ends.

The third column provides the *kañzi* in written semi-cursive style, called *gyoosyo*. This style is characterized by less sharply defined and generally more connected strokes. It is presented in this text for reference only. Do not use this column as your model for writing *kañzi*, at least until you have had extensive writing experience with block-style.

書き順

Kanji #	Block Style (kaisyo)	Stroke Order	Semi-cursive Style (Gyoosyo)
1	一	一	一
2	二	二	二
3	十	十	十
4	日	日	日
5	七	七	七
6	八	八	八
7	九	九	九

Kanji #	Block Style (*kaisyo*)	Stroke Order	Semi-cursive Style (*Gyoosyo*)
8	三	三	三
9	分	分	分
10	六	六	六
11	五	五	五
12	四	四	四
13	本	本	本

KANZI WRITING PRACTICE

	1							
1	一							
2	一	二						
3	一	十						
4	丨	冂	月	日				
5	一	七						
6	ノ	八						
7	ノ	九						
8	一	二	三					

#	1	2	3	4				
9	ノ	八	分	分				
	1	2	3	4				
10	、	亠	六	六				
	1	2	3	4				
11	一	丁	五	五				
	1	2	3	4	5			
12	丨	冂	四	四	四			
	1	2	3	4	5			
13	一	十	才	木	本			

LESSON 9B

14 何　nani /'nan/　　　　　　　　　　what?

N409　nan-　　　　　　　　　　how many ___?; what ___?

何日　　　nan-NITI　　　how many days?; what date?

何分　　　nan-PUN　　　how many minutes? what minute of the hour?

何本　　　nan-BON　　　how many long, cylindrical objects?

1. 何?
2. 何がありますか。
3. 何をしましたか。
4. 何ですか。
5. 何になりたいですか。
6. 何日?
7. 何日ですか。
8. 何日からなんですか。
9. 何日のツアー?
10.何日かかりますか。
11.日本に何日ぐらいいらしたのですか。
12.何分?
13.何分かかりましたか。
14.何分までここにいましたか。

15 下　kuda(sai)　　　　　　　　give [me]

N9

1. 下さい。
2. 六本下さい。
3. もっと下さい。
4. いいのを下さい。
5. 八日までに下さい。

6. それとあれを下さい。

7. おもしろい本を下さい。

8. インタビューしてください。

9. 十分までここにいてください。

Note: Kudasai following a verbal gerund is commonly written in hiragana.

16 千   SEN/'-ZEN/   thousand

N156

三千	SANZEN	3,000
八千	HASSEN	8,000
千本	SEN-BON	1,000 long, cylindrical objects

1. 千

2. 千ページ

3. 三千キロメートル

4. 八千ドルのスポーツカー

5. ここから一千マイルぐらいある。

6. あそこまで二千キロメートルぐらいでしょう。

17 万   MAN   ten thousand

N7

1. 一万

2. 五万三千

3. 四万六千

4. 十万

5. 一千万

6. 一万ドル

7. ほとんど二千万ドルです。

8. あと二千ドルで一万ドルになる。

18 円   EN   (classifier for counting yen); yen

N617

一円	ITI-EN	one yen
四円	YO-EN	four yen
何円	NAN-EN	how many yen?

1. 五千円
2. 一円だけです。
3. 一本千円のペン
4. ほとんど八万円です。
5. もう二千円いるのですが。
6. アメリカまでは一分三十四円です。
7. 一ドルは、円でいくらになりますか。
8. 一万円あったけど、どうしたんでしょう。

19 百 HYAKU/'-BYAKU'-PYAKU/ hundred
N33

三百	SANBYAKU	300
六百	ROPPYAKU	600
八百	HAPPYAKU	800
百万	HYAKUMAN	1,000,000

1. 百
2. 八百
3. 四百六十二
4. 三百五十三
5. 六百九十四
6. 三千五百
7. 千七百四十九
8. 五千百五十円
9. 三百ドルになります。
10. この本は二百ページあります。

20 作 tuku(ru) make
N407

1. 作る。
2. 日本で作りました。
3. おととい作ったんです。
4. テーブルを作ってください。
5. ジョーンズさんが作りました。
6. プラスチックで作ったのですか。

21 今　ima　　　　　　　　　　　now
　　N352　KON
　　　　今日　　　kyoo　　　today
　　　　　or KONNITI　　today (e.g., these days)

1. 今
2. 今から
3. 今まで
4. 今の日本
5. 今します。
6. 今分かりました。
7. 今すぐしましょうか。
8. 今はちょっと分かりません。
9. 今日
10. 今日下さい。
11. 今日しますか。
12. 今日のニュース
13. 今日は二十日です。
14. ミーティングは今日ですね。
15. 今日は。

22 大　oo(kii)　　　　　　　　is big
　　N1171
1. 大きい。
2. 大きいノート

3. 大きくなりました。
4. あまり大きくなりません。
5. もっと大きいのはありませんか。

23 小　tii(sai)　　　　　　　is small
N1355

1. 小さい。
2. 小さいコンピューター
3. あまり小さくありません。
4. 小さいのを作りましょうか。
5. そんなに小さくできるんですか。

24 古　huru(i)　　　　　　　is old (i.e., not new)
N770

1. 古い。
2. 古くなった。
3. とても古い本ですね。
4. 古いウィスキーがある。
5. 古いのは、分かりません。
6. こんなに古いのはだめですよ。
7. このケーキ、ちょっと古くないですか。

25 時　ZI　　　　　　　(classifier for naming o'clock);
N2126　　　　　　　　　　　　time
　　　　　一時　　ITI-ZI　　one o'clock
　　　　　何時　　NAN-ZI　　what time?

1. 二時
2. 一時です。
3. 四時十分からです。
4. 今ちょうど五時です。
5. 今から九時までいます。

6. 何時?
7. 何時ですか。
8. 何時にしましょうか。
9. 何時までにできますか。
10. 何時からここにいますか。
11. コンサートは、何時から何時までですか。

READING WRITING EXERCISES

I. Practice writing responses to the questions in A and B. Follow the pattern shown in the model in each group.

A.

Model: 二百円と三百円でいくらになりますか。

    → 五百円になります。

1. 四千と六千でいくつになりますか。

    →

2. 三千百円と五千六百円でいくらになりますか。

    →

3. 五百ドルと二万ドルでいくらになりますか。

    →

4. 七十二本と三十六本で何本になりますか。

    →

5. 千八十八円と八百三十五円でいくらになりますか。

    →

6. 七万五千と二万八千でいくつになりますか。

    →

B. Choose a suitable interrogative from the selection below. No item in the selection may be used more than once.

Selection: 何本・いくら・何時に・何日まで・何分ぐらい・何時から・何を

Model: ペンがありました。 → 何本あったんですか。

      おつりがいります。 → いくらいるんですか。

1. おととい作りました。 →

2. 今日します。　　　　　　　→

3. 十三日からあそこにいます。　→

4. ここにいらっしゃいますよ。　→

5. ずいぶんかかりますよ。　　　→

II.　Fill in the blanks.

Model:　今三時五十分です。あと ＿＿＿十分＿＿＿ で四時になります。

1. 今一時四十二分です。あと ＿＿＿＿＿ で二時になります。

2. 今四時三十九分です。あと ＿＿＿＿＿ で五時になります。

　　3. 今九時五十四分です。あと ＿＿＿＿＿ で十時になります。

4. 今十一時四十七分です。あと ＿＿＿＿＿ で十二時になります。

5. 今六時二十分です。あと ＿＿＿＿＿ で七時になります。

6. 今五時十五分です。あと ＿＿＿＿＿ で六時になります。

SCANNING EXERCISE

Follow the directions given in Lesson 9A.

書き順

Kanji #	Block Style (kaisyo)	Stroke Order	Semi-cursive Style (Gyoosyo)
14	何	何	何
15	下	下	下
16	千	千	千
17	万	万	万
18	円	円	円
19	百	百	百

Kanji #	Block Style (*kaisyo*)	Stroke Order	Semi-cursive Style (*Gyoosyo*)
20	作	作	作
21	今	今	今
22	大	大	大
23	小	小	小
24	古	古	古
25	時	時	時

KANZI WRITING PRACTICE

	1	2	3	4	5	6	7	
14	ノ	イ	亻	竹	何	何	何	
15	一	丁	下					
16	ノ	ニ	千					
17	一	丁	万					
18	丨	冂	円	円				
19	一	丆	丆	万	百	百		
20	ノ	イ	亻	竹	竹	作	作	
21	ノ	人	今	今				

	1	2	3					
22	一	ナ	大					
	1	2	3					
23	亅	小	小					
	1	2	3	4	5			
24	一	十	六	古	古			
	1	2	3	4	5	6	7	8
25	丨	冂	日	日	旷	旷	昨	昨
	9	10						
	時	時						

LESSON 10A

Some of the expressions introduced in corresponding lessons of JSL can be written in *kanzi* you have learned in previous sections of JWL. These expressions will be listed at the beginning of each section.

New Expression

二十　　　hatati　　　　　　　twenty years of age

26　行　　i(ku)　　　　　　　go
　　N4213

　　　　　行く　　　iku　　　　go

1. 行く。
2. 行きます。
3. 行かない。
4. 行かなかった。
5. 今日は行きたくない。
6. 三時に行ったでしょう。
7. いつ行くんでしょうか。
8. 今日は行かないでしょう。
9. おとといも行かなかったでしょう?

27　人　　hito/'-bito/　　　　　person
　　N339

1. 人
2. その人
3. あの人
4. 大きい人
5. 古い人もいる。1
6. あの人はドイツの人です。
7. この人がブラウンさんです。

1. Note that 古い here means 'experienced' or 'having long career' rather than 'old age'.

8. スミスさんは、どんな人でしょうねえ。

9. ウォーカーさんは、あの人じゃありません。

28 女 onna woman
N1185

1. 女
2. 女の人
3. アルバイトは女の人です。
4. 女の人があちらまで行きました。
5. ジョーンズさんは、女の人でしょう?

29 田 ta/'-da/ field
N2994

Names: 本田　　Honda
　　　　古田　　Huruta
　　　　今田　　Imada
　　　　三田　　Mita
　　　　大田　　Oota

1. 本田です。
2. 今日は三田さんです。
3. 古田さんじゃありませんか。
4. あちらは大田さんでいらっしゃいます。
5. 本田さんも三田さんも二十ぐらいでしょうか。
6. 大田さんは今行きますが、本田さんはあさってまで行きません。
7. 今田さんは女の人ですが、この人じゃありません。

30 山 yama mountain
N1407 SAN/'-ZAN/

Names: 山田　　Yamada
　　　　大山　　Ooyama
　　　　古山　　Huruyama

1. 山
2. 大きい山
3. 山田でございます。
4. 古山さんじゃないですか。
5. 大山さんも五百円あります。
6. セント·ヘレナ山
7. エベレスト山は、どこでしょうか。

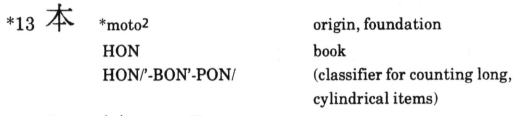

*13 本	*moto²	origin, foundation
	HON	book
	HON/'-BON'-PON/	(classifier for counting long, cylindrical items)

Names:山本　　　Yamamoto
　　　　本山　　　Motoyama

1. 山本さんですね。
2. 山本さん、いらっしゃいますか。
3. 本山さんは、五時にいらっしゃいます。

*23 小	tii(sai)	is small
	*ko	
	*o	

Names:小山　　　Koyama
　　　　　　　or Oyama
　　　　小田　　　Oda

1. 小山さん
2. 小田さんの本
3. 女の小山さんですね。
4. 小田さんと古山さんが行きます。
5. サン·フランシスコの小山さん

2. As noted earlier, the asterisk (*) indicates that this is an additional reading for the kanzi that has already been introduced. The kanzi number indicates where it was first introduced.

6. 小田さんはおととい二十一になった。
7. 山本さんは行ったけど、小田さんはここにいた。

31 子　ko　　　　　　　child
N1264

女の子　　onna no ko　　girl
今日子　　Kyooko　　　(female given name)

1. 女の子
2. お子さん
3. 山田さんのお子さんです。
4. あの子はどこの子でしょうか。
5. 山本さんのお子さんはかわいいですねえ。
6. 小山さんのお子さんでいらっしゃいますか。
7. 今日子ちゃん

*4　日　ka　　　　　(classifier for naming and
　　　NITI　　　　　　counting days)
　　　*hi/'-bi/　　　day
　　　(See Kanzi #32 following.)

32　曜　YOO　　　　　day of the week
N2162

日曜日　　NITIYOObi
or 日曜　　NITIYOO　　Sunday
何曜(日)　NANYOO(bi)　what day of the week?

1. 日曜
2. 今日は何曜日?
3. 日曜日に作りました。
4. 日曜日は二十日ですね。
5. 小山さんは日曜日に行きました。

33 火 KA   fire

N2743

        火曜(日)   KAYOO(bi)   Tuesday

1. 火曜日
2. 今日は火曜です。
3. 火曜日に行きたい。
4. 火曜までにしてください。
5. 火曜日には分かるでしょう。
6. 日曜日から火曜日までの三日
7. 山本さんが火曜日の二時にいらっしゃいます。

34 土 DO   earth, soil

N1050

        土曜(日)   DOYOO(bi)   Saturday
        土、日   DO·NITI   Sat-Sun

1. 土曜
2. 土曜日のコンサート
3. これは土曜日に古山さんが作りました。
4. 土、日
5. 土、日だけ、一つ千円です。
6. 土、日はオフィスにおりません。

35 木 MOKU   tree, wood

N2170

        木曜(日)   MOKUYOO(bi) Thursday
        火、木   KAA·MOKU   Tues-Thurs
        火、木、土   KAA·MOKU·DOO Tues-Thurs-Sat

1. 木曜日
2. 今日から木曜まで
3. 木曜日は小山さんです。
4. 木曜日にいらっしゃいます。

5. 火曜は古山さんで、木曜は本田さんです。
6. 火、木、土
7. 火、木、土のクラス
8. 火、木はいるけれど、土曜はいません。
9. 火、木は九時からで、土、日は十一時からです。

36 休 yasu(mu) rest, take time off
　　N380　yasu(mi) vacation; holiday; time off
　　　　　休む　　　yasumu　　rest; take time off
　　　　　（お)休み　(o)yasumi　vacation; holiday; time off

1. 休む。
2. 休みます。
3. 四日休んだ。
4. 土、日も休まなかった。
5. 十分ほど休みましょうか。
6. 休み
7. 休みの日
8. 今日は休みだ。
9. お休みは何曜日ですか。
10. 六日は木曜だけど、休みになります。
11. 土曜日はお休みだけど、今日はミーティングがあるんです。

37 男 otoko man
　　N2996
　　　　　　男の子　　otoko no ko　　boy

1. 男
2. 男の子
3. 男のアルバイト
4. 三田さんの男の子
5. 男の人も女の人もいました。
6. 火曜日は男の小山さんで、木曜日は女の小山さんです。

*22 大　　oo(kii)

　　　　*DAI

　　　　(See Kanji 38 following.)

38　学　　GAKU　　　　　　　　　　study; learning

　　N1271

　　　　　大学　　　　DAIGAKU　　　college, university

1. 大学
2. 大学に行く。
3. 大学はどちらですか。
4. 今日から大学が休みだ。
5. 大田さんは今、大学です。
6. 日曜は休みだけれど、大学に行きました。

READING SELECTION

This is part of an essay.

　　　今日は土曜日で休みだけれど、山本さんは大学まで行きます。五日から大学のキャフェテリアでアルバイトをしているのです。山本さんの大学にはキャフェテリアが三つありますが、山本さんは小さいキャフェテリアでキャッシャーをしています。アルバイトは火、木、土で、火、木は九時から十一時までですが、今日は二時から六時までです。

Note: キャフェテリア is more innovative than カフェテリア.

READING WRITING EXERCISES

I. The following is a chart of people assigned to run a booth at an exhibit. Answer the questions below on the basis of the chart.

DATE	Tue 3	Wed 4	Thu 5	Fri 6	Sat 7	Sun 8
	Ms. Honda	Ms. Honda	Ms. Honda	Ms. Honda		Ms. Honda
	Mr. Yamada		Mr. Yamada		Mr. Yamada	
					Mr. Ooyama	
		Mr. Mita	Mr. Mita	Mr. Mita	Mr. Mita	Mr. Mita
		Ms. Yamamoto		Ms. Yamamoto		Ms. Yamamoto

1. 三日は何曜日ですか。

2. 土曜日は何日ですか。

3. 木曜日はだれがいますが。

4. 本田さんは男の人ですか。

5. 山田さんはいつですか。

6. 三田さんは何日から何日までいますか。

7. 山本さんはいつが休みですか。

8. 本田さんは、休みの日がだくさんありますか。

9. 木曜はだれが休みますか。

10. 山田さんは何日休みますか。

11. 山田さんは何日に休みますか。

12. 火曜日は山田さんだけですか。

13. 男の人は山田さんだけですか。

14. 土曜日は女の人だけですか。

15. 大山さんは何曜日ですか。

II. Answer the following questions in English in as much detail as you can on the basis of the content of the Reading Selection

1. What day of the week is it today?

2. Why is Yamamoto going to the university today?

3. How long has s/he been doing this?

4. Describe Yamamoto's work schedule.

5. How many cafeterias are there on campus?

SCANNING EXERCISE

In the classified section of a currrent newspaper, scan for all employment opportunities that are written in *katakana*, or in a combination of *katakana* and Roman letters. Determine if the particular position is for a male, a female, or unspecified.
Write ten such sequences in Japanese and give their English equivalents. Indicate gender specifications, if any.

書<ruby>か</ruby>き順<ruby>じゅん</ruby>

Kanji #	Block Style (kaisyo)	Stroke Order	Semi-cursive Style (Gyoosyo)
26	行	行	行
27	人	人	人
28	女	女	女
29	田	田	田
30	山	山	山
31	子	子	子
32	曜	曜	曜

Kanji #	Block Style (kaisyo)	Stroke Order	Semi-cursive Style (Gyoosyo)
33	火	火	火
34	土	土	土
35	木	木	木
36	休	休	休
37	男	男	男
38	学	学	学

KANZI WRITING PRACTICE

	1	2	3	4	5	6		
26	ノ	ク	彳	彳	彳	行		
27	ノ	人						
28	く	女	女					
29	丶	冂	四	甲	田			
30	丨	山	山					
31	フ	了	子					

	1	2	3	4	5	6	7	8
32	丨	冂	日	日	日コ	日コ	日ヨ	日ヨ
	9	**10**	**11**	**12**	**13**	**14**	**15**	**15**
	日羽	日羽	曜	曜	曜	曜	曜	曜
	17	**18**						
	曜	曜						

	1	2	3	4
33	丶	丷	少	火

	1	2	3
34	一	十	土

	1	2	3	4
35	一	十	才	木

	1	2	3	4	5	6
36	ノ	亻	仁	什	休	休

	1	2	3	4	5	6	7
37	丶	冂	四	用	田	罗	男

	1	2	3	4	5	6	7	8
38	丶	丷	丷	灬	学	学	学	学

LESSON 10B

39 出 de(ru)　　　　　　　　attend; go out, leave
　　N97

1. 出る。
2. 出ない。
3. 今出ています。
4. おとといも出なかった。
5. 今日のクラスには出ない。
6. あさってのゼミに山本さんも出る?

40 口 kuti/'-guti　　　　　　　mouth
　　N868

	出口	deguti	exit
Names:	山口	Yamaguti	
	田口	Taguti	
	出口	Deguti	

1. 出口
2. 出口はどこですか。
3. 出口から出てください。
4. ここは、出口じゃありません。
5. このビルの出口は三つございます。
6. 山口さんも本田さんも女の人ですよ。
7. 田口さんは今日いらっしゃらないでしょう。

41 入 i(ri)
　　N574

　　　　　　入り口
　　or 入口　　　　iriguti　　　entrance

Note: *iri* is a special stem form which is used within compounds such as *iriguti*. It does not combine with the *-masu* ending to form a distal style verbal predicate.

1. 入り口
2. 入り口と出口
3. むこうの入り口
4. 入り口はあそこです。
5. このビルの入り口はどこでしょうか。

42 毎 MAI   every ---
N2467

毎日   **MAINITI**   every day

1. 毎日
2. 毎日行きます。
3. 大学は毎日ですか。
4. 毎日三時からの休み
5. 毎日三時から十五分休む。
6. 毎日六時から七時まで休む。
7. そのゼミは毎日じゃありません。
8. 大学が休みの日も毎日アルバイトをしています。

43 月 tuki   moon; month
N2169 GETU

(ka)GETU   (classifier for counting months)

GATU   (classifier for naming months);
                                  month

毎月   **MAIGETU**
        or MAItuki   every month
月曜(日)   GETUYOO(bi)   Monday
一か月   IK-kaGETU   one month
何か月   nan-kaGETU   how many months?

一月	ITI-GATU	January
	or hito-tuki	one month
何月	nan-GATU	what month?
今月	KONGETU	this month

Note: The *ka* in *-kagetu* may be written with か, or with カ or ケ in reduced form.

1. 毎月
2. 毎月行きます。
3. 毎月二十日に出る。
4. 山田さんは毎月四日休む。
5. ミーティングは、毎月します。
6. 月曜
7. 月曜日のゼミ
8. 月、火は休みじゃありません。
9. 今月
10. 今月の八日
11. あのパーティーは今月でしたか。
12. 今月の二十四日は大学は休みです。
13. 今月はコンサートがたくさんあります。
14. 一か月
15. 一か月の休み
16. もう一ヵ月いたい。
17. あと一ヵ月だけですね。
18. 何ヵ月ぐらいかかるでしょうか。
19. 今日でちょうど二ヵ月になります。
20. 一月と二月
21. 七月と八月の休み
22. 大学は四月からです。
23. 五月十日は木曜日ですか。
24. 何月までいらっしゃいますか。
25. 十月までにはいらっしゃるでしょう。
26. 一月います。

27. 一月かかるでしょう。

28. アパートは一月いくらですか。

44 来 ku(ru)   come

    N202   ki(ta)   came, has come

               ko(nai)   doesn't come, won't come, hasn't come

               RAI   coming

               来月   RAIGETU   next month

Note: Following a verbal gerund (as in 行って), this verbal is commonly written in hiragana.

1. 来る。

2. いつ来る?

3. 毎月来るでしょう。

4. 来た。

5. 行ってきませんませんか。

6. アルバイトが来ている。

7. 土曜日にも来てください。

8. 山口さんはおとといも来た。

9. 来ない。

10. 来なかった。

11. 男の人は来なかった。

12. 本田さんは来なかったんです。

13. 来月

14. 今月と来月

15. 来月のコンサート

16. 来月は28日までです。

17. 来月もいらっしゃるでしょう。

45 水 SUI   water

    N2482

水曜(日)	SUIYOO(bi)	Wednesday
月、水	GES·SUI	Mon.-Wed.
水、木	SUI·MOKU	Wed.-Thur.

1. 水曜日
2. 水曜日のゼミは出ない。
3. 水曜日に来てくださいませんか。
4. 月、水
5. 月、水は十時からです。
6. 水、木はここにおりません。

46 金 KIN  gold; metal
N2482

金曜(日)	KINYOO(bi)	Friday
月、水、金	GES·SUI·KIN	Mon.-Wed.-Fri.

1. 金曜
2. 金曜日
3. 金曜日の二時
4. 山本さんは金曜日もいらっしゃるでしょうか。
5. 月、水、金は四時からアルバイトです。
6. 月、水、金のクラス
7. 月、水、金は大田さんで、田口さんは火、木、土です。
8. 金、土、日が休みなんです。

47 知 si(ru) know
N3169

1. 知る。
2. よく知っている。
3. あまりよく知らない。
4. うちの子は知りません。
5. 本田さんを知っています。
6. 小田さんがよく知っています。

7. 大きいビルだけど、知らなかったんです。

48 生　　SEI　　　　　　　　　　　　　birth; life
　　N2991
　　　　　学生　　　　GAKUSEI　　student
　　　　　大学生　　　DAIGAKUSEI　college student

1. 学生
2. ここの学生
3. 学生のアルバイト
4. アルバイトの学生
5. 女の学生も男の学生も来た。
6. 大学生
7. 大学生がよく行く。
8. 大学生になりました。

49 先　　saki　　　　　　　　　　　　ahead
　　N571　SEN
　　　　　先生　　　　SENSEI　　　teacher; doctor
　　　　　先月　　　　SENGETU　　last month

1. 先
2. 先のほう
3. 入り口の先
4. 大学はこの先です。
5. もっと先にあります。
6. この先まで行ってください。
7. 先生
8. 山田先生
9. 古田先生の本
10. 先生のお子さん
11. 先生がいらっしゃらないんですが...
12. 先月

13. 先月作りました。
14. 先月から毎日来ています。
15. 先月も今月も休んでいましたが、来月からまた来ます。
16. 先月まで二千円だったけど、来月から二千五百円になります。

50 見 mi(ru) — look at
N4284 mi(seru) — show
mi(eru) — appear; be visible

1. 見る。
2. よく見てください。
3. そんな本は見なかった。
4. 見ましたか、田口さんの本。
5. 今、となりでテレビを見ています。
6. 本を見たけれど、やっぱり分からなかった。
7. 見せる。
8. 子どもに見せた。
9. あの本を見せてください。
10. 山田先生にもお見せしたいですね。
11. すみませんが、ちょっと見せてくださいませんか。
12. 小山さんには見せたけど、田口さんには見せなかった。
13. 見える。
14. 先生が見えました。
15. 山本先生は見えませんでした。
16. 来月はどなたがお見えになりますか。
17. 田口先生は、今月は見えなかったけど、来月はいらっしゃるでしょう。

READING SELECTION

This is a memo found at school.

　田口先生へ
　日本大学の山本先生は、来月の十二日(水)にい
らっしゃいます。金曜日まで、毎日こちらにお見
えになります。金曜日の六時から、レセプション
がありますが、先生もいらっしゃいませんか。ゼ
ミの学生も来ます。
　　　　十月二十日　　　　　本田

READING WRITING EXERCISES

I. Practice writing the responses to the cues. Follow the pattern shown in the model in each group.

A.   **Model:** 火曜日にしますか。   → 火曜日にはしないでしょう。

      1. 水曜日に来ますか。   →

      2. 今日作りますか。   →

      3. 山本さんに見せましたか。   →

      4. あさっても休みますか。   →

      5. お子さんも見えましたか。   →

      6. あの女の人が知っていますか。   →

B.   **Model:** 火曜日にしましたね。   → 火曜日にはしなかったでしょう。

      1. 八日にも来ましたね。   →

      2. ここで見ましたね。   →

      3. ゼミに出ましたね。   →

      4. 先生もお作りになりましたね。   →

5. 毎月行きましたね。　　　　→

6. 二か月いましたね。　　　　→

C.　　Model: 三日は火曜日ですね。　→ 火曜日じゃないでしょう。

1. 今日は十日ですね。　　　　→

2. デパートはもっと先ですね。　→

3. お休みは四月ですね。　　　→

4. 月、水、金はゼミですね。　→

5. アルバイトは毎日ですね。　→

6. 出口はあそこですね。　　　→

D.　　Model: 三日は火曜日でしたか。　→ 火曜日じゃなかったでしょ
　　　　　　　　　　　　　　　　　　　う。

1. そこは入り口でしたか。　　→

2. 女の人も学生でしたか。　　→

3. 大学は火、木でしたか。　　→

4. 先生はお休みでしたか。　　→

5. おとといは山口さんでしたか。　→

6. 金曜は三時からでしたか。　　　　→

II. Answer the questions IN ENGLISH on the basis of the content of the Reading Selection.

1. Who wrote this memo? When?

2. To whom is this memo addressed?

3. Who is this memo about? (Give details)

4. When is the reception?

5. Who else is going to be at the reception?

6. What does こちら (underlined) refer to?

SCANNING EXERCISE

Using the same job advertisements you chose in Section A, determine the working conditions by scanning for working days and hours as well as for monthly salary if specified. Write down the information using *kanzi*, *hiragana*, and *katakana* as appropriate. Write the name of the job if it is written in *katakana*).

書き順

Kanji #	Block Style (*kaisyo*)	Stroke Order	Semi-cursive Style (*Gyoosyo*
39	出	出	出
40	口	口	口
41	入	入	入
42	毎	毎	毎
43	月	月	月
44	来	来	来

Kanji #	Block Style (*kaisyo*)	Stroke Order	Semi-cursive Style (*Gyoosyo*)
45	水	水	水
46	金	金	金
47	知	知	知
48	生	生	生
49	先	先	先
50	見	見	見

KANZI WRITING PRACTICE

	1	2	3	4	5			
39	丨	屮	屮	出	出			

	1	2	3					
40	丨	冂	口					

	1	2						
41	丿	入						

	1	2	3	4	5	6		
42	丿	𠂊	仁	每	每	每		

	1	2	3	4				
43	丿	刀	月	月				

	1	2	3	4	5	6	7	
44	一	丆	㝵	立	半	来	来	

	1	2	3	4				
45	亅	才	水	水				

	1	2	3	4	5	6	7	8
46	丿	人	亼	今	仐	余	金	金

		1	2	3	4	5	6	7	8
47		ノ	⺊	⺦	矢	矢	知	知	知
		1	2	3	4	5			
48		ノ	⺀	牛	牛	生			
		1	2	3	4	5	6		
49		ノ	⺀	牛	生	牛	先		
		1	2	3	4	5	6	7	
50		丨	冂	冃	月	目	貝	見	

LESSON 11A

*27 人　hito/'-bito/　　　　　　　　　person

　　　　*ri
　　　　*NIN
　　　　*ZIN

一人	hito-ri	one person, single person
二人	huta-ri	two people
三人	SAN-NIN	three people
四人	yo-NIN	four people
アメリカ人	amerikaZIN	an American
何人	nan-NIN	how many people?
or	nani-ZIN	what nationality?
大人	otona	an adult

1. 一人
2. 二人来ました。
3. 一人で作りました。
4. 今日は何人見えますか。
5. お子さんは何人いらっしゃいますか。
6. 男の人が四人と、女の人が六人います。
7. スミスさんと山本さんと、三人で行きたいのです。
8. あの人は何人?
9. アメリカ人の大学生
10. 大人
11. 大人は一人千五百円でございます。

51 間　aida　　　　　　　　　　　interval, space between

N4949 KAN

時間	ZIKAN	time
一時間	ITI-ZIKAN	one hour
何時間	nan-ZIKAN	how many hours?

間 -*KAN* also occurs as a suffix with numbers. The numbers by themselves can indicate either a point in time or a duration of time, but the alternant with suffix 間 -*KAN* has the durational meaning only.

Examples:

二日　hutu-ka 'two days' or 'second of the month'

二日間 hutu-kaKAN 'two days'

五分　GO-HUN 'five minutes' or 'minute five of the hour'

五分間　GO-HUNKAN 'five minutes'

1. 間
2. こことそこの間
3. その大きいビルの間
4. ワシントンとサン・フランシスコの間にある。
5. 時間
6. 時間がなかった。
7. 時間はどのぐらいかかる?
8. そんなに時間がかかるんですか。
9. コンサートの時間が分からないんですが。
10. 一時間
11. 四時間ぐらい
12. 二時間とちょっと
13. テレビを二時間見た。
14. 三時間ぐらいかかるでしょう。
15. 何時間?
16. あと何時間ぐらいかかる?

52 週 SYUU   week

N4707

来週	RAISYUU	next week
毎週	MAISYUU	every week
今週	KONSYUU	this week
先週	SENSYUU	last week

| 一週間 | IS-SYUUKAN | one week |
| 何週間 | nan-SYUUKAN | how many weeks? |

1. 来週
2. 来週山に行く。
3. 来週は休みだから来ない。
4. 今日から来週の月曜日までいる。
5. 毎週
6. 毎週水、金に作ります。
7. 毎週のフットボールのゲーム
8. 山本さんのお休みは、毎週木曜日です。
9. 今週
10. 今週のゼミ
11. 今週までのお休み
12. 先週
13. 先週作った。
14. 先週は金曜日に行った。
15. アルバイトは先週から来ている。
16. 一週間
17. 二週間毎日行った。
18. 三週間だけのアルバイト
19. 一週間ぐらい休んで、十日から大学に出た。
20. アメリカは、今日でちょうど六週間になります。
21. 何週間?
22. 何週間の休み?
23. 日本に何週間いましたか。
24. あさってで何週間になる?

53 待 ma(tu)   wait, wait for
N1609

1. 待つ。
2. 何分待った?

3. 待ちたくない。
4. 待ってください。
5. 待っていてください。
6. お待ちになったでしょう。
7. 本山さんを待っています。
8. 出口のそばで待ちましょう。
9. 八時までは待っていますから。
10. もう五分だけ待ちましょうか。
11. 時間がないからあんまり待ちたくない。

54 午 GO   noon
    N162   (See Kanzi 55 and 56)

56 前 mae   front; before
    N595   ZEN
       午前   GOZEN   morning, A.M.
       前田   Maeda   (family name)

1. 前
2. 前の入り口
3. 古山さんの前
4. 入り口の前でお待ちしております。
5. 四日前
6. 前のアルバイト
7. 十分ほど前にできました。
8. 八時ちょっと前までいらっしゃった。
9. 午前
10. 午前八時
11. 午前のミーティング
12. 午前十一時二十八分
13. 午前七時のニュースを見たい。
14. 前田さん

15. 前田さんが待っています。

56 後　usi(ro)　　　　　　　　　　　　back, rear

　　N1610　ato

　　　　　GO

　　　　午後　　　GOGO　　　　afternoon, P.M.

1. 後ろ
2. ビルの後ろ
3. 後ろから見た。
4. 前にも後ろにもある。
5. もっと後ろに行ってください。
6. 後ろからだったから、よく分からなかった。
7. 後
8. また後で。
9. 後で見せてください。
10. 二時間ぐらい後になります。
11. 午後
12. 午前と午後
13. 午後四時三十五分
14. 午後五時からのクラス
15. 午後まではおりませんから...
16. 午前も午後も時間がありません。

57 年　tosi　　　　　　　　　　　　year

　　N188　NEN　　　　　　　　(classifier for naming and
　　　　　　　　　　　　　　　counting years); year

　　　　(ka)NEN　　　　　　　(classifier for counting years)
　　　　今年　　kotosi　　　this year
　　　　来年　　RAINEN　　　next year
　　　　毎年　　MAItosi
　　　　or MAINEN　　　　　every year

一年	ITI-NEN	one year
二年	NI-NEN	two years; the year two
何年	nan-NEN	what year?; how many years?
一ゕ年	IK-kaNEN	one year
二ゕ年	NI-kaNEN	two years
何ゕ年	nan-kaNEN	how many years?
一年間	ITI-NENKAN	one year
二年間	NI-NENKAN	two years
何年間	nan-NENKAN	how many years?

Note:

(1)   The *ka* of *kaNEN* is written with か, カ, or ヶ in reduced form.

(2)   -年間 is a more commonly occurring alternant than -ゕ年 for counting years.

1. 今年
2. 今年から
3. 今年の学生は三百人だ。
4. 今年の四月に大学を出た。
5. 来年
6. 来年まで
7. 来年から大学に行く。
8. 毎年
9. 毎年お見えになる。
10. 毎年八月は休みだ。
11. 一年
12. 1990年
13. 千九百八十年から今年まで
14. ドイツに三年いて、それからスイスに五年いました。
15. ここには1986年に来たから、もうすぐ3年になる。
16. 何年?
17. 二千年まであと何年?
18. ヨーロッパに何年から何年までいましたか。
19. 一年間

20. 六年間かかって大学を出ました。
21. 何年間
22. 何年間のプログラムだろうか。

58 食 ta(beru)   eat
N5154

1. 食べる。
2. 何が食べたい?
3. もっと食べない?
4. 毎日何時に食べますか。
5. あの男の子はよく食べますねえ。
6. アイスクリームが食べたくなった。

59 方 kata↑   person
N2082 HOO/'-BOO'-POO/   direction; alternative
☆前方1   ZENPOO   forward, frontward

1. 女の方
2. その男の方
3. 先週は、そんな方は見えませんでした。
4. アメリカ人の女の方がいらっしゃいました。
5. フランス人の女の方がお待ちになっていらっしゃいます。
6. 後ろの方
7. 前の方にあります。
8. ホテルはこちらの方ですね。
9. ニューヨークはどちらの方だろう。

60 雨 ame/'ama-'-same/   rain
N5042

1. 雨

1. The blank star (☆) symbol designates a supplementary example that the student is not required to memorize.

2. 雨の日曜日

3. 今日は雨だ。

4. あさっても雨だろうね。

5. 午後から雨になるでしょう。

6. 雨だったから行きたくなかった。

7. すごい雨ですけど、やっぱり行きましょう。

61 会　　a(u)　　　　　　　　　　meet

N381　KAI/'-GAI/

(See Kanzi 62, following)

会田　　　Aida　　　(Family name)

1. 会う。

2. インド人に会った。

3. 入り口の前で会いませんか。

4. あの人にはおととい会いました。

5. 大山先生にお会いになりましたか。

6. そんな人には会わなかったけど...

7. 会田さん

8. 会田さんと今田さん

9. あの方は会田さんじゃありませんか。

62 社　SYA　　　　　　　　　　a company

N3231

会社	KAISYA /'-GAISYA/	a business company
＋ガス会社	gasuGAISYA	gas company
＋大会社	DAIGAISYA	a large company
☆子会社	koGAISYA	a subsidiary company

1. 会社

2. 会社の人

3. その会社

4. シカゴの会社
5. 会社で会った。
6. 休みで会社に行かなかった。
7. 毎日七時までには会社に出る。
8. 前は小さかったけど、なかなか大きい会社になった。
9. ガス会社
10. 大会社のサラリーマン
11. うちは、そんな大会社じゃありません。

63 思 omo(u)   think
N3001
1. 思う。
2. そう思った。
3. いいと思います。
4. 前に会ったと思う。
5. かわいいと思いませんか。
6. この会社をどう思いますか。
7. 先週の月曜は雨だったと思います。
8. 小山さんに分かるとは思わなかった。
9. あの方はイギリス人だと思いましたが。

READING SELECTION

This is part of a letter Ms. Maeda received.

前田さん
　　日本は、先週から毎日雨です。ロンドンはどう
ですか。
　　今、大学にイギリス人の学生が五人来ていま
す。今年からのプログラムで、一年日本にいま
す。日本からも来年からは毎年学生が行くんです
よ。イギリスには前に行きましたけど、一週間だ
けだったから、このプログラムでまた行きたいと
思っています。前田さんはロンドンに何年までい
ますか。そちらで会いたいですね。
・
・
・

　　では、さようなら。

　　六月二十八日

　　　　　　　　　今田みち子

READING WRITING EXERCISES

I. Practice writing responses to the questions in A and B. Follow the pattern shown in the model in each group. In each response, choose an appropriate item from the selection given. No item may be used more than once.

A.

Selection: 今日・ナイフとフォーク・二十人・カナダ・四週間ぐらい・
メキシコ人・会社

Model: それはいつしますか。　　　　→　今日するだろうと思います。

1. 何で食べますか。　　　　　　→

2. どのぐらいかかりますか。　　→

3. 何人が来ましたか。　　　　　→

4. 先生は何人いらっしゃいますか。　→

5. ミーティングはどこですか。　→

6. 大学はどこでしたか。　　　　→

B.

Selection:　　　雨だ・みんな休んでいる・六時まで会社にいる・先週のだ・
知らなかった・今年はだめだ・二時間ぐらいかかる

Model: どうして行かないのでうか。　　→　雨だからです。

1. このケーキ、どうして食べないのですか。

2. どうして来なかったのですか。
　　　→

3. ミーティングはどうしてできないのですか。
　　　→

4. どうして六時まで来ないのですか。
　　　→

5. どうして来年になったのですか。
　　　→

6. どうしてバスで行かなかったのですか。
　　　→

II. Answer the following questions in Japanese.

1. 今年は何年ですか。

2. 今日は、何月何日何曜日ですか。

3. 今、何時ですか。午後ですか。

4. 水曜日と金曜日の間は何曜日ですか。

5. 毎日何時間ぐらい大学にいますか。

6. 今の大学に、あと何年ぐらいいますか。

7. 来年の二月ごろ、どこにいると思いますか。

8. 先週の水曜日は雨でしたか。

9. あなたの先生は日本人ですか。

10. あなたのクラスには学生が何人ぐらいいますか。

11. あなたのクラスの学生は、みんなアメリカ人ですか。

III. Answer the questions IN ENGLISH in as much detail as you can on the basis of the content of the letter in the Reading Selection.

1. Who wrote the letter to whom?

2. Where is the writer? The recipient?

3. How does the writer describe the weather in Japan?

4. What special event at school is reported? (Give details)

5. What does the writer want to do next year? Why?

6. What question does the writer have about the recipient?

7. In what connection is this question raised?

8. What does そちら (underlined) refer to?

SCANNING EXERCISE

Obtain a pamphlet written in Japanese, or select from a current Japanese magazine or newspaper an advertisement for a packaged tour to places the names of which are written in *katakana*, and scan for the following information. Write what you have found out in Japanese and give its English equivalent.

1.   Which places are included in the tour?

2.   How many days is the tour?

3.   When do you leave? When do your return?

4,   Which hotel(s) will you be staying at?

5.   How much does the tour cost?

6.   Are there any optional side tours in addition to what is already part of the package? What are the details on time, place and cost?

書き順

Kanji #	Block Style (kaisyo)	Stroke Order	Semi-cursive Style (Gyoosyo)
51	間	間	間
52	週	週	週
53	待	待	待
54	午	午	午
55	前	前	前
56	後	後	後
57	年	年	年

Kanji #	Block Style (*kaisyo*)	Stroke Order	Semi-cursive Style (*Gyoosyo*)
58	食	食	食
59	方	方	方
60	雨	雨	雨
61	会	会	会
62	社	社	社
63	思	思	思

KANZI WRITING PRACTICE

	1	2	3	4	5	6	7	8
51	丨	冂	尸	尸	阝	門	門	門
	9	**10**	**11**	**12**				
	門	閒	間	間				
52	丿	刀	月	用	用	用	周	周
	9	**10**	**11**					
	周	週	週					
53	丿	彳	彳	行	彳	往	往	待
	9							
	待							
54	丿	乍	乍	午				
55	丶	丷	丷	产	肖	肖	肖	前
	9							
	前							

	1	2	3	4	5	6	7	8
56	丿	⺅	彳	彳	彳	徭	徉	後

	9							
	後							

	1	2	3	4	5	6		
57	丿	𠂉	上	午	乍	年		

	1	2	3	4	5	6	7	8
58	丿	人	亼	今	今	仐	食	食

	9							
	食							

	1	2	3	4				
59	丶	亠	方	方				

	1	2	3	4	5	6	7	8
60	一	冂	冋	雨	雨	雨	雨	雨

	1	2	3	4	5	6		
61	丿	人	仐	合	会	会		

	1	2	3	4	5	6	7	
62	丶	ラ	ネ	ネ	ネー	社	社	

	1	2	3	4	5	6	7	8
63	丨	冂	皿	田	田	思	思	思

	9							
	思							

LESSON 11B

64 駅　EKI　　　　　　　　　　　station

N5199

　　　　　　駅前　　　EKImae　　area in front of the station

1. 駅
2. 駅の前
3. ここの駅
4. 大学の前の駅
5. どの駅ですか。
6. 駅の出口で待っていた。
7. 駅まで行ってください。
8. 駅で待っておりますから。
9. 駅の前でタクシーを待ちましょう。
10. 駅前
11. 駅前のスーパーマーケット

65 名　na　　　　　　　　　　　name

N1170

　　　　　　名前　　　namae　　　name

1. 名前
2. お名前は?
3. 先生の名前
4. 名前を知っている。
5. 駅の名前が分からない。

66 朝　asa　　　　　　　　　　　morning

N3788

　　　　　　毎朝　　　MAIasa　　every morning
　　　　　　今朝　　　kesa　　　this morning

朝子　　　　Asako　　　　(female given name)

1. 朝
2. 朝見た。
3. 朝のニュース
4. あさっての朝はおりません。
5. 毎朝
6. 毎朝八時までに来る。
7. 毎朝ジョギングしたい。
8. アルバイトは、毎朝九時からだ。
9. 山本さんも毎朝このバスだろうと思う。
10. 今朝
11. 今朝の雨
12. 今朝何食べた?
13. 今朝は会社に行きたくない。
14. 今朝、駅で山田さんに会った。

67 安　yasu(i)　　　　is cheap
N1283

Names:安田　　　Yasuda　　　(family name)
　　　　安子　　　Yasuko　　　(female given name)

1. 安い。
2. 安い本
3. とても安かった。
4. そんなに安いとは思わなかった。
5. もっと安くならないでしょうか。
6. 安田さん
7. 会社の安田さん
8. 安子さんの会社はどこですか。

68 私　watakusi 'watasi　　　I, me
N3265

1. 私
2. 私の先生
3. 本山さんと私
4. 私から出ます。
5. 私、会田でございます。
6. 私も今朝十時に来ました。
7. 本田さんと私と二人で行く。
8. 私も午後までここにいるのですか。

69 父 titi   father

    N2832 too

         お父さん   otoosan ↑   father

1. 父
2. 父と私
3. 父の名前
4. 今朝の父
5. 父からのメッセージ
6. 父の会社が大きくなった。
7. お父さん
8. お父さんのお名前
9. これ、お父さんの本だろう?
10. お父さんが待っていらっしゃいます。

70 母 haha   mother

    N2466 kaa

         お母さん   okaasan ↑   mother

1. 母
2. 父と母
3. 母の大学
4. 母が作りました。
5. 父と母と二人だけで行きました。

6. お母さん
7. お母さんに会いましたよ。
8. お母さんに、どうぞよろしく。
9. あの人、古田さんのお母さんじゃありませんか。
10. 来週のパーティーには、お母さんもお出になるでしょう?
11. お父さんはよく知っているけど、お母さんには今日はじめて会いました。

71 **外** hoka   other, another

    N1168 GAI

       外人   GAIZIN   foreigner

1. 外
2. 外に何か。
3. 外の人は来月も来ます。
4. これはだめだからすぐに外のを作ります。
5. 山本先生は見えたが、外の先生は見えない。
6. 外人
7. 外人の学生
8. あの外人、だれ?
9. 女の外人さんがいらしています。
10. 外人だから知らないと思ったけど、よく知っていた。

72 **困** koma(ru)   become distressed, annoyed,

    N1033   troubled

1. 困る。
2. 困りましたねえ。
3. 父も母も困っております。
4. 毎日雨で、困っただろうと思う。
5. 名前が分からなくて困った。
6. 小さい会社だからドルが安くなって困っている。

73 晩 BAN night

N2145

今晩	KONBAN	tonight
毎晩	MAIBAN	every night

1. 晩
2. 朝と晩
3. 晩の七時
4. 金曜日の晩
5. 晩八時に出た。
6. そのミーティングは晩ですよ。
7. 朝はここで食べるけれど、晩は会社で食べる。
8. 今晩
9. 今晩は。
10. 今晩作ります。
11. 今晩はちょっと困ります。
12. 今晩の何時からしましょうか。
13. 今晩から来週の水曜日までワシントンにいます。
14. 毎晩
15. 毎晩見る。
16. 毎晩二時間ぐらいします。
17. 毎晩六時から七時までいる。

74 旅 RYO travel

N2088

(See Kanzi 75, following)

75 館 KAN building

N5174

旅館	RYOKAN	Japanese-style inn
会館	KAIKAN	assembly hall, clubhouse

1. 旅館

2. 安い旅館

3. 旅館の名前

4. 駅のすぐ前の旅館

5. 大田旅館はこの先です。

6. あそこは旅館でしょうか。

7. 毎年ホテルだけど、今年は旅館だろう。

8. 古い大きい旅館で、外人もよく来ます。

9. 駅から旅館までマイクロバスで十分ぐらいかかった。

10. 小さい旅館ですが、サービスはなかなかいいと思います。

READING SELECTION

This is a letter Yasuko received.

安子さん

　　今日は。そちらの毎日はどうですか。私は八月から会社に行っていますが、このアルバイトはあまりおもしろくありません。今はまあまあですけど、一週間ほど前までは外のアルバイトをしたいと思っていました。毎朝七時からなんですよ。まあ、土曜が毎週お休みですから、いいのですが...

　　安子さんはテレビを見ますか。来週の木曜日に父が出るんですよ。6チャンネルの晩八時からのドキュメンタリーで、タイトルは「日本の旅館」だったと思います。父の旅館も今年で七十年ですから、古い旅館になるのですね。今は、駅のすぐそばに大きいホテルができて父は困っています。でも、日本人はホテルに行くけど、父の旅館には外人さんがよく来るんですよ。おもしろいでしょう?日本に来ているのだから、旅館のほうがおもしろいと思うのでしょうね。それに、うちの旅館はすごく安いから。あ、旅館の名前は山水(さんすい)です。ドキュメンタリー、見てくださいね。

　　では、大山先生にもどうぞよろしく。さようなら。

　　　　八月十八日

　　　　　　　　　　　　　　山本朝子

READING WRITING EXERCISES

I. Write in Japanese what corresponds to the descriptions given.
Model: 今の時間   <u>八時二十五分</u>

1. アメリカの大きい駅   _____

2. お父さんの名前   _____

3. 安いレストラン   _____

4. 外人の男の名前   _____

5. 朝のニュース   _____

6. 七日間   _____

7. 今日の朝   _____

   8. アメリカ人の先生の名前   _____

   9. 日本の会社   _____

10. 今年   _____

II. Practice writing responses to the questions. Follow the pattern shown in the model. In each response, choose an appropriate item from the selection given. No item may be used more than once.

Selection: 今田さん・父・旅館・駅の前・あの外人の名前・雨になった・毎晩・後ろの方

Model: だれが分かるんでしょうか。　→　今田さんが分かるだろうと思います。

1. どこで待ったんでしょうか。　　→

2. どうして困ったんでしょうか。　→

3. あそこは何なんでしょうか。　　→

4. だれに見せたんでしょうか。　　→

5. いつ来るんでしょうか。　　　　→

6. 何を知らないんでしょうか。　　→

7. どこから見たんでしょうか。　　→

III. Answer the questions IN ENGLISH in as much detail as you can on the basis of the content of the letter in the Reading Selection.

1.　What has the writer been doing since August?

2.　What two things about her job does the writer mention as the source of her discontent?

3.   Who does the writer mention in connection with a TV program?

4.   Describe the program in detail. When is it? What channel is it on?
      What kind of program is it? What is it about?

5.   What does the writer's father do?

6.   Why is he troubled?

7.   What phenomenon does the writer describe as amusing?

8.   How does the writer account for this phenomenon?

9.   What is 'Sansui?'

10. What does the writer invite the recipient of the letter to do?

11. In what connection is Ooyama mentioned? Who could it be?

12. When was this letter written?

13. What is the writer's name?

14. What does the underlined indicate?

15. How would you describe the tone of this letter? Is it friendly? Business-
      like?

IV. Write a similar letter to a pen pal in Japan. Include the following:

1. Question as to how your pen pal's school is going;

2. Description of your part-time work at the university cafeteria;

3. Information concerning your mother's appearance on a TV news program last week (your mother has been running a small business of homemade ice cream for the past 20 years);

4. Inquiry as to how many hours your pen pal watches TV everyday;

5. Closure giving your regards to your pen pal's mother;

6. Date and your name.

Note:

(1) Start every new paragraph with an indentation one space.

(2) Allow the same amount of space for '、 ' and '。 ' as for other letters.

(3) Do not try to use symbols you have not learned. You should be able to write this letter using only the *kanzi* you have learned, *katakana*, and *hiragana*.

SCANNING EXERCISE

Follow the directions given in Lesson 11A.

Kanji #	Block Style (kaisyo)	Stroke Order	Semi-cursive Style (Gyoosyo)
64	駅	駅	駅
65	名	名	名
66	朝	朝	朝
67	安	安	安
68	私	私	私
69	父	父	父

Kanji #	Block Style (*kaisyo*)	Stroke Order	Semi-cursive Style (*Gyoosyo*)
70	母	母	母
71	外	外	外
72	困	困	困
73	晩	晩	晩
74	旅	旅	旅
75	館	館	館

KANZI WRITING PRACTICE

	1	2	3	4	5	6	7	8
64	一	厂	厂	圧	匡	馬	馬	馬

	9	10	11	12	13	14		
	馬	馬	馬ㄱ	馬ㄱ	駅	駅		

	1	2	3	4	5	6		
65	ノ	ク	夕	夕	名	名		

	1	2	3	4	5	6	7	8
66	一	十	广	市	古	直	直	草

	9	10	11	12				
	朝	朝	朝	朝				

	1	2	3	4	5	6		
67	ヽ	⼧	宀	宀	安	安		

	1	2	3	4	5	6	7	
68	ノ	⼆	千	千	禾	私	私	

	1	2	3	4				
69	ノ	八	分	父				

	1	2	3	4	5		
70	ㄥ	母	母	母	母		

	1	2	3	4	5		
71	ノ	ク	夕	列	外		

	1	2	3	4	5	6	7
72	｜	冂	冂	冊	困	困	困

	1	2	3	4	5	6	7	8
73	｜	冂	月	日	日	日	日	昀
	9	10	11	12				
	晚	晚	晚	晚				

	1	2	3	4	5	6	7	8
74	丶	亠	方	方	方	扩	扩	旅
	9	10						
	旅	旅						

	1	2	3	4	5	6	7	8
75	ノ	人	今	今	今	今	食	食
	9	10	11	12	13	14	15	16
	食	食	館	館	館	館	館	館

LESSON 12A

76 東　TOO　　　　　　　　　　　east
N213

(SeeKanzi 77, following)

77 京　KYOO　　capital
N295

東京	TOOKYOO	Tokyo
東京駅	TOOKYOO-EKI	Tokyo Station
東京大学	TOOKYOO-DAIGAKU	Tokyo University
東大	TOODAI	Tokyo University
京大	KYOODAI	Kyoto University
京子	Kyooko	(female given name)

1. 東京
2. 東京の人
3. 東京の大学
4. 母が東京に来ている。
5. 東京まで、何時間かかるだろう。
6. 東京駅
7. 東京駅の前の会社
8. 東京駅までタクシーで行った。
9. 東京大学
10. 東京大学の先生がいらっしゃった。
11. 東大を出ました。
12. 朝は東大にいました。
13. 東大の学生はみんな来ました。
14. 京大へ行きたいと思っている。
15. 東大の学生ですか、京大の学生ですか。
16. 京子さんからのメッセージ
17. 田中京子さんといいます。

18. 東京駅で、京子さんのお父さんにあった。

78 校 KOO　　　　　　　　　　　　　school
N2260
　　　　　　学校　　　　GAKKOO　　　school

1. 学校
2. 学校の名前
3. 東京の大きい学校
4. 女だけの学校がある。
5. 今日は学校に行きたくない。
6. 山本さんは、今日も学校に来なかった。
7. 月曜から金曜までは毎日学校に行っている。

79 高 taka(i)　　　　　　　　　is expensive, is high
N5248 KOO
　　　＋ 高校　　　　KOOKOO　　　　high school
　　　＋ 高校生　　　KOOKOOSEI　　a high school student
　　　　 高山　　　　Takayama　　　(family name)
　　　　 高田　　　　Takada　　　　(family name)
　　　　 高　　　　　Takasi　　　　(male given name)
　　　　 高子　　　　Takako　　　　(female given name)

1. 高い。
2. 高い山
3. 高い大学
4. 高い?安い?
5. そんなに高くない。
6. すごく高いレストランだと思った。
7. 高校
8. 高校の先生
9. アメリカの高校を出た。
10. 高校はこちらですか、むこうですか。

11. 高校は日本で行きましたが、大学はフランスでした。
12. 高校生
13. 高校生が八人いる。
14. 高校生?大学生?
15. アメリカからの高校生
16. 高校生二人と大学生三人の五人で来た。
17. 高山さんの会社
18. 母の名前は京子で、父は高です。
19. 高田さんは高田京子さんという。
20. 京子さんも高子さんも、東京をよく知りません。

80　兄　ani　　　　　　　　older brother
N875　nii
　　　（お)兄さん　(o)niisan↑　　　older brother

1. 兄
2. 兄の名前
3. 兄は高という。
4. 兄は今月二十八になる。
5. 兄は今年の四月から東大に行っている。
6. お兄さん
7. お兄さんでしたか。高田さんでしたか。
8. お兄さんは何人いらっしゃいますか。
9. お兄さんは何とおっしゃいますか。

81　姉　ane　　　　　　　　older sister
N1207　nee
　　　（お)姉さん　(o)neesan↑　　　older sister

1. 姉
2. 兄と姉
3. 東京の姉
4. 姉が作った。

5. 姉が二人おりまして...

6. 姉は高子といいますが。

7. お姉さん

8. お姉さんに会いましたよ。

9. 兄、または姉がおりますから。

10. お姉さんの会社の人じゃありませんか。

11. お姉さんにそうおっしゃってください。

82 書 ka(ku)　　　　　　　　write; draw
N3719

1. 書く。

2. 何を書いた?

3. 書かなかった。

4. 一人で書きました。

5. もっときれいに書きましょう。

6. ここに名前を書いてください。

7. ノートに書きますから待ってください。

8. これはお父さんがお書きになったのですか。

9. 書きますから、ゆっくりおっしゃってください。

83 言 i(u)　　　　　　　　say
N4309

Note: When *iu* means 'be called' or 'be named,' it is regularly written in *hiragana*.

Example: 山本といいます。　'I'm called Yamamoto.'

1. 言う。

2. 言った?

3. 名前を言わなかった。

4. 私にはそう言いましたよ。

5. あまり言いたくないけれど...

6. 高山さんにも言ってください。

7. 学生には来週言いましょう。

84 店　mise　　　　　　　　shop
N1509

1. 店
2. 古い店
3. 駅の前の高い店
4. どのお店がいいですか。
5. あの店はパンケーキハウスという。
6. 大きい店にはあると思ったけど、やっぱりなかった。
7. この店もいいけれど、あっちの店はもっと安いと思います。

85 半　HAN　　　　　　　　half
N132

一時半	ITI-ZI-HAN	1:30
一日半	ITI-NITI-HAN	one day and a half
一年半	ITI-NEN-HAN	one year and a half
半時間	HANZIKAN	half hour
半日	HANNITI	half day
半年	HANtosi	half year
半田	Handa	(family name)

1. 一時半
2. 三時半からのゼミ
3. 朝七時半はラッシュアワーだ。
4. 五時または五時半にいらしてください。
5. 一日半
6. シカゴには一日半だけいた。
7. このコピーは、一日半かかりますよ。
8. 一年半
9. 一年半かかって書いた。
10. 日本に来て、まだ一年になりませんん。

11. 半時間
12. もう半時間でできますから。
13. 半日
14. 日本は半日ぐらい先です。
15. 半年
16. 来週でちょうど半年になります。
17. このコースは半年のコースですか、一年のコースですか。
18. どなたが半田さんですか。
19. 半田さんはお姉さんもお兄さんも二人ずついます。

86 手 te/'-de/   hand
N1827
手前   temae   this side [of]

1. 手
2. 大きい手
3. きれいな手ですね。
4. ちょっと手を見せてください。
5. 手で書きましたか。タイプしましたか。
6. 手前
7. 駅の手前
8. 手前の方の出口
9. もっと手前にもいい店があります。

87 紙 kami/'-gami/   paper
N3510
手紙   tegami   letter

1. 紙
2. 小さい紙
3. 紙で作った。
4. この紙はいりません。
5. この紙に書いてくださいませんか。

6. 手紙
7. だれからの手紙?
8. 手紙を待っている。
9. 毎週母に手紙を書いた。
10. 高田さんからの手紙、見た?
11. ヨーロッパの姉から手紙が来た。
12. この手紙は二時間半かかって書きました。

	白	siro/'-ziro/	white
88			
N3095		siroi(i)/'sira-/	is white
	白	siro*	white color
	白田	Sirota	(name)
	白山	Siroyama	(name)

Note: Adjectival color words like *siroi, akai, aoi, kiiroi,* and *kuroi* have nominal alternants *siro, aka, ao, kiiro,* and *kuro,* respectively. These nominal color words may be used interchangeably with their adjectival alternants in some cases. Thus:

白い紙 or 白の紙   'white paper'

However, they have various special uses which distinguish them from the adjectivals, including the following:

(a)   only nominals are used to NAME the colors. Thus:

白がいいです。   'White is good.' (i.e., the color white)
白のがいいです。   'The white one is good.' (i.e., an object that is white)

(b)   only the nominals are used when an object is described by several colors. Thus:

白いセーター   'a white sweater'
白とピンクのセーター   'a blue-and-pink sweater'
白いセーターとピンクのセーター   'a white sweater and a pink sweater'

(c)　　only the nominals are themselves described by adjectivals.

きれいな白です。　　　　　　　　　'[It]'s a pretty white.'

1. 白

2. 白がいい。

3. 白ワイン、ありますか。

4. 白い。

5. 白い紙

6. あまり白くない。

7. これも白くするのですか。

READING SELECTION

This is a memo left by Ms. Furuta.

田口さん
　来週東京大学の今田先生がいらっしゃいます
が、私はあさってからニューヨークへ行って、来
月の十日まで会社には来ませんから、今田先生に
そうおっしゃってください。
　お会いしたいけれど、残念(ざんねん)です。
　どうぞよろしくおっしゃってください。

　　11月25日
　　　　　　　　　古田

READING WRITING EXERCISES

I.Practice writing responses to the questions in A and B. Follow the pattern shown in the model in each group.

A.

Model: コピー、しましたか。 　　　→ 　　いま高山さんがしています。

1. メモ、書きましたか。 　　　→

2. コーヒー、作りましたか。 　　　→

3. 先生に会いましたか。 　　　→

4. 本、見ましたか。 　　　→

5. ミーティングに出ましたか。 　　→

B.

Mode: 　　高田さんはおととい来ました。

　　　　　→ 　　高田さんはおとといから来ています。

1. 会社の名前は二年前に知りました。

　　　　　→

2. 半田さんは先週あちらに行きました。

　　　　　→

3. このワープロは今朝だめになりました。

　　　　　→

4. 先生は一週間半前にお見えになりました。

　　　　　→

5. 旅館の名前は月曜日に分かりました。
　　　　→

6. 京子さんは今年の二月に来ました。
　　　　→

II. Following the pattern shown in the model, fill in the blanks with appropriate expressions to make the responses meaningful. (Note the use of the extended predicate.)For each blank, choose an appropriate item from the selection given and make necessary adjustments in its form. No item may be used more than once.

Selection:　　　食べる・作る・見る・思う・する・書く・見せる・待つ・休む

Model:「何をしていたんですか。」
　　　　→　　「ケーキを食べていたんです。」
1.「何をしているんですか。」
　　　　→　　「大学のカタログを＿＿＿＿＿＿＿＿。」

2.「何をしていたんですか。」
　　　　→　　「雨で困ったと＿＿＿＿＿＿＿＿。」

3.「何をしていたんですか。」
　　　　→　　「パスポートを＿＿＿＿＿＿＿＿。」

4.「何をしているんですか。」
　　　　→　　「手紙を＿＿＿＿＿＿＿＿。」

5.「何をしていたんですか。」
　　　　→　　「ちょっと＿＿＿＿＿＿＿＿。」

6. 「何をしているんですか。」
 　　　　→　　「山本さんを＿＿＿＿＿＿＿＿。」

7. 「何をしているんですか。」
 　　　　→　　「パイを＿＿＿＿＿＿＿＿。」

8. 「何をしていたのですか。」
 　　　　→　　→「インタビューを＿＿＿＿＿＿＿＿。」

III. Answer the questions in Japanese.

1. 　今東京にいますか。

2a. 学校に行っていますか。

 b. その学校は大学ですか。

3. 　あなたの学校は何といいますか。

4a. 今週手紙を書きましたか。

 b. 何ページ書きましたか。

5a. お兄さんがいますか。

 b. 何といいますか。

 c. お姉さんは?

6a. そばに店がありますか。

b.　その店には紙がありますか。

c.　その店の名前は何といいますか。

7.　半年前はどこにいましたか。

IV. Answer the following questions IN ENGLISH in as much detail as you can on the basis of the memo in the Reading Selection.

1. When did Furuta write this memo?

2. To whom is the memo addressed?

3. When is Imada coming?

4. Where does Imada work?

5. In what connection is New York mentioned?

6. Why can't Furuta meet Imada? (Give details)

7. How does Furuta feel about it?

8. What does Furuta request?

SCANNING EXERCISE

Obtain a copy of a resume, and scan for the following information concerning the applicant's educational background and family. Answer the following questions IN ENGLISH on the basis of the resume:

1. When did the applicant enter high school?

2. When did the applicant finish high school?

3. Has the applicant gone to college?

4. Does the applicant live with her/his parents?

5. Does the applicant have any elder siblings? If yes, how many? Brother(s) or sister(s)? Are any of her/his family members employed by a company?

書き順

Kanji #	Block Style (kaisyo)	Stroke Order	Semi-cursive Style (Gyoosyo)
76	東	東	東
77	京	京	京
78	校	校	校
79	高	高	高
80	兄	兄	兄
81	姉	姉	姉
82	書	書	書

Kanji #	Block Style (kaisyo)	Stroke Order	Semi-cursive Style (Gyoosyo)
83	言	言	言
84	店	店	店
85	半	半	半
86	手	手	手
87	紙	紙	紙
88	白	白	白

KANZI WRITING PRACTICE

	1	2	3	4	5	6	7	8
76	一	厂	厅	百	百	車	東	東

	1	2	3	4	5	6	7	8
77	丶	亠	亠	立	古	亨	京	京

	1	2	3	4	5	6	7	8
78	一	十	才	木	术	杧	栌	朾

	9	10						
	柠	校						

	1	2	3	4	5	6	7	8
79	丶	亠	亠	古	古	古	高	高

	9	10			
	高	高			

	1	2	3	4	5
80	丶	口	口	尸	兄

	1	2	3	4	5	6	7	8
81	人	夕	女	女	妒	妁	姉	姉

	1	2	3	4	5	6	7	8
82	ヲ	ヲ	ヨ	聿	聿	書	書	書

	9	10						
	書	書						

	1	2	3	4	5	6	7	
83	丶	亠	言	言	言	言	言	

	1	2	3	4	5	6	7	8
84	丶	亠	广	广	庁	庄	店	店

	1	2	3	4	5			
85	丶	ソ	半	半	半			

	1	2	3	4	5			
86	ノ	二	三	手				

	1	2	3	4	5	6	7	8
87	乙	幺	幺	糸	糸	糸	紅	紙

	9	10						
	紙	紙						

	1	2	3	4				
88	ノ	イ	白	白	白			

LESSON 12B

89 話　　hana(su)　　　　　　　　talk
N4358　hanasi　　　　　　　　　　a talk
　　　WA
　　　(See Kanzi 90, following)

1. 話す。
2. 先生と話した。
3. ゆっくり話してくださいませんか。
4. 九時半ごろまで話した。
5. 話
6. 山田さんの話
7. 兄の話をしています。
8. おもしろい話ですね。
9. 大学の話をなさいました。

90 電　　DEN　　　　　　　　　　electricity
N5050

　　　電話　　　DENWA　　　telephone

1. 電話
2. お電話です。
3. 電話で話した。
4. 会社からの電話
5. 前にも後ろにも電話がある。
6. 東京大学の高山先生から電話がありました。
7. 電話する。
8. 後でまたお電話します。
9. 大田さんに電話なさいましたか。
10. 五時半までに電話してください。
11. 何時に電話をかけましょう。

12. 学校から電話をかけてくださいませんか。

13. 山口さんにおとといの朝、電話がありました。

91 車　kuruma　　　　　　　car

N4608 SYA

電車　　　　DENSYA　　　electric train

1. 車

2. ドイツの車

3. 白い小さい車

4. 車で行きましょう。

5. この車は先生のです。

6. 電車

7. 電車で来ました。

8. 電車の方が安いでしょう。

92 赤　aka　　　　　　　　red

N4534 aka(i)　　　　　　　is red

赤　　　　aka　　　　red color

赤ちゃん　akatyan　　　baby

赤電話　　akaDENWA　　public (i.e. red) telephone

1. 赤

2. その車は赤ですか。

3. 赤と白のストライプ

4. 赤い。

5. 赤くなりましたね。

6. 赤い紙と白い紙

7. 赤ちゃん

8. かわいい赤ちゃんですね。

9. どなたの赤ちゃんですか。

10. 三月に姉に赤ちゃんができました。

11. 赤電話

12. あれは赤電話じゃありません。
13. 赤電話は入り口の方にあったと思います。

*56 後　usi(ro)　　　　　　　back, rear
　　　　　ato　　　　　　　　later, afterward
　　　　　*noti　　　　　　　later, afterward
　　　　　GO
　　　　後ほど　　notihodo　　later

1. 後ほど
2. 後ほどまた。
3. 後ほどいらして下さい。
4. 後ほどお電話いたします。

93 明　MYOO　　　　　　　light, bright
　　N2110
　　　　明日　　　asita
　　　　　or MYOONITI　　tomorrow
　　　　明後日　　MYOOGONITI　day after tomorrow

1. 明日来る?
2. 明日もあさっても学校だ。
3. 明日のゼミには姉も出ると思う。
4. 今日は来ないけど明日は来るだろう。
5. 明日でございますか。
6. 明日からは東京におりません。
7. 明日もテニスをなさいますか。
8. 今日は山田先生がいらっしゃいますが、明日はどなたでしょうか。
9. 明後日
10. パーティーは明後日でございます。
11. 明後日からのコンテストにお出になりますか。
12. 明日いらっしゃるけれど明後日はいらっしゃらないんですね。

94 屋 ya   dealer, seller;
N1392   business establishment

| 本屋 | HONya | bookstore; bookdealer |
| 山本屋 | Yamamoto-ya | Yamamoto's (establishment) |

1. 本屋
2. 古い大きい本屋
3. あの店は本屋ですね。
4. 本屋の前で待っています。
5. 駅の前のアイスクリーム屋
6. あの旅館は山本屋といいます。
7. 「もしもし、山本屋でございます。」

*24 古 huru(i)   is old
*KO/'-GO/

| 名古屋 | naGOya | Nagoya |

1. 名古屋
2. これから名古屋へ?
3. 東京と名古屋の間
4. 名古屋の古い店
5. 来週は名古屋に行っています。
6. 名古屋の高校に二年ほど行っていました。
7. ここから名古屋まで、車でどのぐらいかかりますか。

95 買 ka(u)   buy
N3637

1. 買う。
2. 何を買ったの?
3. 六万円のを買いました。
4. 先週の金曜日に買いました。
5. 見たけど、高かったから買わなかった。
6. ドルで買いましたか、円で買いましたか。

7. 二本買いたかったけど、一本だけになりました。

8. 赤い紙は買ったけど、白いのは買わなかった。

9. 学校のそばの本屋でアガサ・クリスティの本を買った。

10. 一本三百円のを二本買ったから、あつりは四百円でした。

96 友 tomo　　　　　　　　friend
N858

友だち	tomodati	friend
友田	Tomoda	(family name)
大友	Ootomo	(family name)
友子	Tomoko	(female given name)

1. 友だち

2. 友だちと話した。

3. 日本の古い友だち。

4. 明日、友だちに会う。

5. 友だちと二人で行った。

6. 古い車を友だちから買った。

7. ドイツ人の友だちができた。

8. 名古屋から友だちが来ている。

9. 友だちの車でシカゴまでドライブした。

10. 友田先生は明日こちらにお見えになります。

11. 友子さんが買ったから私も買いたくなった。

97 参 mai(ru)↓　　　　　　go; come
N850

1. 参ります。

2. 明日参ります。

3. 行って参ります。

4. 車で参りましょう。

5. 兄も、姉も参りません。

6. 母が一人で参りますから。

7. 何時に参りましょうか。
8. 今年もお休みはメキシコに参ります。

98 用　YOO　　　　　　　business, matter to attend to
　　N2993
　　　　(See Kanzi 99, following)

99 事　koto/'-goto/　　　act, fact, matter
　　N272　ZI
　　　　(See Kanzi 100, following)
　　　　用事　　　YOOZI　　business, matter to attend to
　　　　火事　　　KAZI　　　fire

1. 用事
2. 会社の用事
3. 用事がある。
4. どんな用事でしょうか。
5. 用事があって電話した。
6. ここの用事はこれだけです。
7. その用事は後でいいでしょう?
8. 名古屋で用事がございまして、明日から参ります。
9. 用事はないけれど、大友さんに会いたくなって来たんです。
10. 火事
11. 火事になった。
12. 火事でびっくりしました。
13. 先週学校で火事があったのです。
14. どうして火事になったのでしょうね。

100 仕　SI/'-ZI/　　　　　doing
　　N362
　　　　仕事　　　sigoto　　　work

1. 仕事

2. おもしろい仕事
3. 仕事の話で電話した。
4. 年後、仕事で人に会う。
5. こんな仕事はしたくない。
6. じゃあ、どんな仕事がしたい?
7. お仕事はどちらでなさいますか。
8. 仕事でオレゴンに来ております。。
9. 三年前から今の会社で仕事をしています。
10. お父さんはどんな仕事をしていらっしゃるんですか。
11. 日曜日だけど仕事があるから、これから会社に行ってきます。

READING SELECTION

This is a fax message Ms. Furuta sent.

8/20　　10 a.m.

大友さん

　　山口さんからの手紙のコピー、ありがとうございました。
明後日は、私も用事で東京まで出ますから、お会いして、お話
ししたいと思います。山口さんは一人でいらっしゃるのでしょ
うか。前はお姉さんもいらっしゃったと思いますが。

　　名古屋からの電車の時間は分かりますか。車で駅まで参り
ましょうか。

　　今日は午後八時ごろまで会社で仕事していますから、お電
話下さい。お待ちしております。

　　　　　　　　　　　古田高子

READING WRITING EXERCISES

IA. Fill in the blanks with the appropriate items from the selection. **No item may be used more than once.**

Selection: 手紙・赤いペン・兄の車・電話・小さい本屋・仕事・三人

1. ＿＿＿＿＿＿＿ で書きました。

2. ＿＿＿＿＿＿＿ で話しました。

3. ＿＿＿＿＿＿＿ で買いました。

4. ＿＿＿＿＿＿＿ で言いました。

5. ＿＿＿＿＿＿＿ で参りました。

6. ＿＿＿＿＿＿＿ で行きました。

7. ＿＿＿＿＿＿＿ で作りました。

1B. Provide English equivalents for the completed phrases in Section A above.

II. Practice writing responses to the questions in A and B. Follow the pattern shown in the model in each group.

A.
Model: 山田さんが来ました。 → 先生もいらっしゃいました。

1. 山口さんがしました。 →

2. 大田さんが行きました。 →

3. 山本さんが買いました。 →

4. 本田さんが書きました。 →

5. 友田さんが待っています。 →

6. 前田さんができます。 →

7. 大前さんが分かります。 →

8. 田口さんが困っています。 →

9. 半田さんが会います。 →

B.
Model: ゴルフしますか。 → いえ、姉はいたしますが。

1. 五分ぐらい待ちますか。 →

2. いいと思っていますか。 →

3. 電話しますか。 →

4. 仕事がありますか。　　　　　→

5. 駅まで行きますか。　　　　　→

6. 先生に手紙を書きますか。　　→

7. 先生に見せますか。　　　　　→

III.　Answer the following questions in Japanese.

1a.　明日は何日ですか。

 b.　何曜日ですか。

2a.　車がありますか。

 b.　何年のですか。

3.　学校まで電車で行きますか。

4a.　今週、ダウンタウンで、用事がありますか。

 b.　その用事は時間がかかりますか。

5a.　友だちがいますか。

 b.　何人いますか。

 c.　アメリカ人ですか。

6a.　そばに本屋がありますか。

b. 何といいますか。

c. 古い店ですか。

d. よくそこで買いますか。

IV. Answer the following questions IN ENGLISH in as much detail as you can on the basis of the fax message in the Reading Selection.

1. When did Furuta send this message?

2. To whom did Furuta send the message?

3. What does Furuta thank this person for?

4. What information did the letter apparently contain?

5. Does Furuta live in Tokyo? How do you know?

6. What does she want to do the day after tomorrow?

7. What is Furuta wondering about? Why?

8. What does Furuta already know about the train?

9. What additional information does Furuta want?

10. What does Furuta offer to do?

11. What does Furuta request?

12. In what connection is the company mentioned?

V.   Write a similar fax message to Ms. Tomoda, a business acquaintance in Japan. In it, you should:

1.   Indicate the time and the date of the message;

2.   Indicate the name of the person to whom the messsage should be delivered;

3.   Acknowledge with gratitude the letter Ms. Tomoda sent you last week;

4.   Confirm your understanding that Ms. Tomoda is going to San Francisco next month;

5.   Inform her that you, too, are going to be there on business, and that (you think) you will be at the Hilton Hotel from the third until the sixth;

6.   Inquire if Ms. Tomoda knows the name of her hotel in San Francisco;

7.   Inform her that since you have some business to attend to on Thursday and Friday but have time on Saturday, you would like to meet and talk with her then;

8.   Indicate that you will be where you are through this month, and request that she send (give) you a fax;

9.   Sign your name in full.

Remember: You can write this message using only the grammatical patterns and expressions you have learned so far. No extra *kanzi* should be necessary either.

SCANNING EXERCISE

Follow the directions given in Lesson 12A.

書き順

Kanji #	Block Style (kaisyo)	Stroke Order	Semi-cursive Style (Gyoosyo)
89	話	話	話
90	電	電	電
91	車	車	車
92	赤	赤	赤
93	明	明	明
94	屋	屋	屋

Kanji #	Block Style (*kaisyo*)	Stroke Order	Semi-cursive Style (*Gyoosyo*)
95	買	買	買
96	友	友	友
97	参	参	参
98	用	用	用
99	事	事	事
100	仕	仕	仕

KANZI WRITING PRACTICE

	1	2	3	4	5	6	7	8
89	ヽ	亠	士	言	言	言	言	言
	9	**10**	**11**	**12**	**13**			
	訂	訐	訐	訐	話			

	1	2	3	4	5	6	7	8
90	一	厂	冂	市	雨	雨	雨	雨
	9	**10**	**11**	**12**	**13**			
	雰	雫	雫	雪	電			

	1	2	3	4	5	6	7
91	一	冖	冂	百	百	亘	車

	1	2	3	4	5	6	7
92	一	十	土	赤	赤	赤	赤

	1	2	3	4	5	6	7	8
93	⎸	冂	月	日	日	明	明	明

	1	2	3	4	5	6	7	8
94	フ	コ	尸	尸	居	居	居	屋
	9							
	屋							

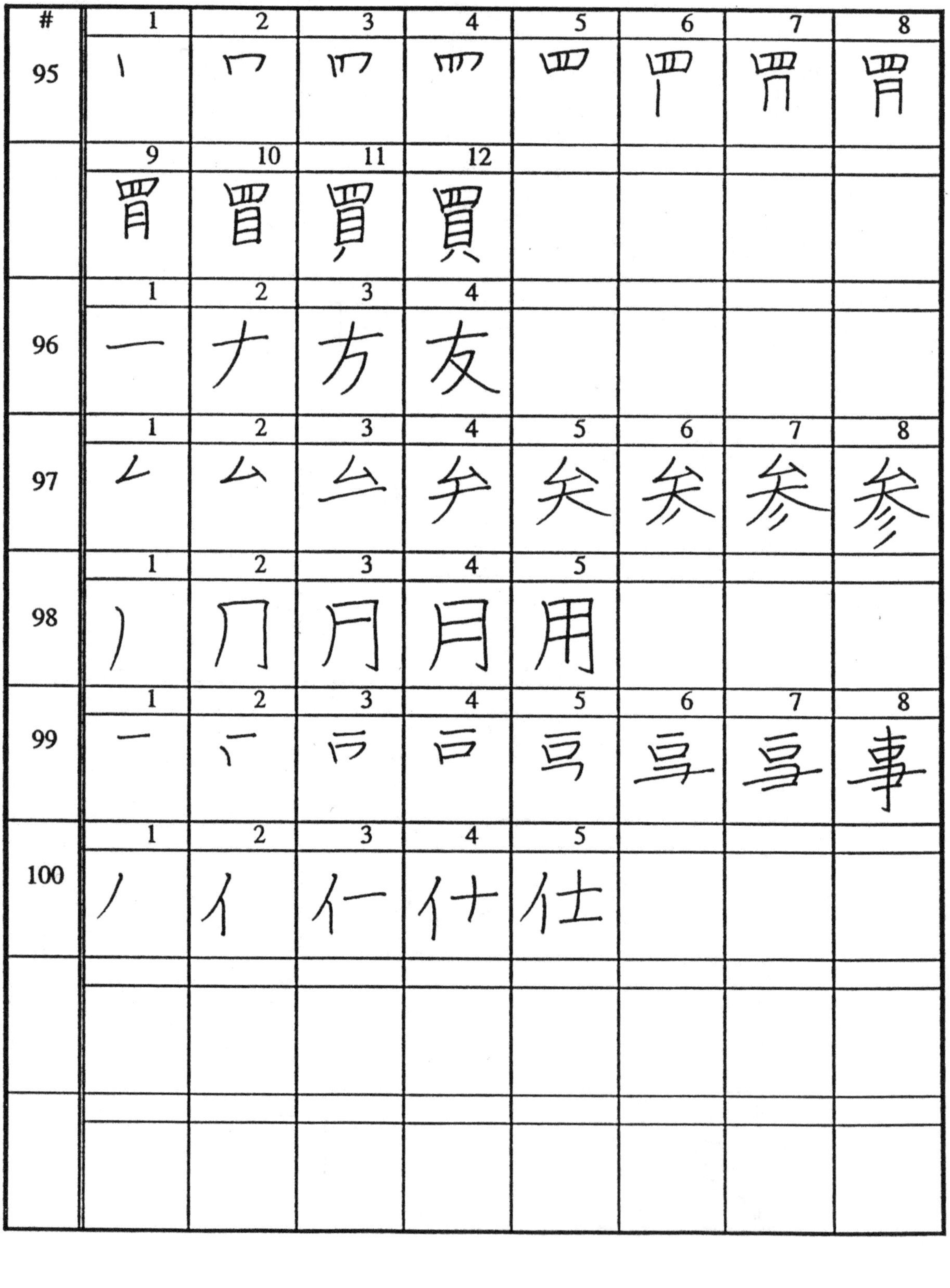

#	1	2	3	4	5	6	7	8
95	丶	冖	罒	罒	四	罒	罒	胃
	9	10	11	12				
	胃	冒	買	買				
	1	2	3	4				
96	一	ナ	方	友				
	1	2	3	4	5	6	7	8
97	ㄥ	ム	台	�	矣	叁	参	参
	1	2	3	4	5			
98	)	几	月	月	用			
	1	2	3	4	5	6	7	8
99	一	亍	戸	戸	亐	亖	亖	事
	1	2	3	4	5			
100	ノ	イ	仁	什	仕			